CONFERENCES

an organiser's guide

PETER COTTERELL

Hodder & Stoughton

A MEMBER OF THE HODDER HEADLINE GROUP

DEDICATION

This book is dedicated to all those in the industry who have resisted using the word 'professional' as a self-description.

May their dignity and judgement be richly rewarded.

British Library Cataloguing in Publication Data

Cotterell, Peter
  Conferences: Organiser's Guide
  I. Title
  060.68

  ISBN 0 340 56794 5

First published 1994
Impression number   10   9   8   7   6   5   4   3   2   1
Year   1998   1997   1996   1995   1994

Typeset by Serif Tree, Kidlington, Oxon
Printed in Great Britain for Hodder & Stoughton Educational, a division of Hodder Headline PLC, Mill Road, Dunton Green, Sevenoaks, Kent TN13 2YA by St Edmundsbury Press Ltd.

CONTENTS

ACKNOWLEDGEMENTS

This book is based on many experiences, both mine and others'. Several people helped significantly by reading chapters and offering improvements, or being interviewed.

Thank you Ann James of the Radio Academy; Jocelyn Marsh of the British Public Works Association; David Seekings, author of *How to organise Successful Conferences and Meetings*; Caroline Sumner of Meetings Management; John Winkler of Winkler Marketing; Peter Worger of the Association of Conference Executives (ACE); and Robin Young of the Smoke House Conference Centre.

Others helped by supplying material, thoughts and ideas over the years.

Thank you Mike Adams, Elaine Adlam, Verite Baker, Jackie Billings, Richard Birchnall, Steven Brown, Tony Carey, Peter Chester, Tim Chudley, Ken Clayton, Peter Cox, Max Cuff, Owen Davey, Derek Deere, Wendy Farr, John Fraser-Robinson, Sandra George, Geoffrey Grey-Forton, Sheila Hayles, Michael Henderson, John Hiett, Ken Jennings, Richard John, Alan Jowett, Albert Kemp, Gordon Kennedy, Sue Langabeer, Martin Lewis, Jane Morrison, Peter Longbottom, Mike Pattison, John Plews, Caroline Pocock, Mike Prager, Peter Rand, Nick Robinson, Tony Rogers, Paul Rouse, Tony Russell, Ann Rust, Cristina Stuart, Derek Taylor, Ken Taylor, Stewart Vassie, Bryn Williams and Larry Wilson.

Thanks are also due to Margaret Fitch, who typed the manuscript and to my long-suffering family, Pauline, Malcolm and Owen, who relinquished the dining room table and put up with an increasingly wild-eyed and manic scribbler as deadlines drew nearer.

INTRODUCTION

I am having a funny dream ...

I'm attending a one-day seminar on a subject that really interests me. The venue is a high class hotel in Central London.

I arrive full of enthusiasm at 0830 hours for an 0900 hours start. The organiser's staff are just unpacking the boxes of brochures, delegate packs and badges. The organiser can be heard in the adjoining room shouting at someone because the room has not been laid out as agreed 'months ago'.

Coffee arrives at 0840 hours with jam doughnuts. As I bite into one, some red jam squirts down the front of my white shirt. I go to the cloakroom to wash it off. The revolving towel has not been replaced and the dangling end is wet and dirty. I rub my shirt front dry with blue toilet paper and the colour comes off. Red and blue make purple.

The first session is due to start at 0900 hours but doesn't get going till 0920 hours because the first speaker, who arrives at 0850 hours, demands to know why the overhead projector (OHP) he specified is not set up.

About one hundred of us file into the meeting room at 0920 hours. It is small, has a low ceiling, a pillar in the middle and no natural light. The rather worn and very hard banqueting chairs are laid out theatre style and very close together. The person on my left is rather large and had something with garlic and chilli for dinner last night. The person on my right lights up a cigarette. The person in front of me is also rather large and, since the screen is only one metre off the floor due to the low ceiling, I can only see the top quarter of it. As it transpires it really doesn't matter.

The speaker starts by telling a smutty joke that was on television last night and then tells us about a book he's written, 'signed copies of which will be available afterwards'. He reads from a script and shows a selection of pages from his book, on the OHP. It is awfully boring. He over-runs his new alloted time by 20 minutes but not before he reminds us again that signed copies of his book are actually available for us to purchase. No one buys any and he quickly leaves.

Despite us being late out of the first session the coffee has not arrived when we break for the morning beverage. The organiser, looking very cross, runs off to find the hotel banqueting manager. Coffee arrives 10 minutes later and is set up on one large table with the milk, sugar and biscuits alongside. There is only one person serving and the start of the next session is announced before everyone has been served. The garlic and chilli person next to me takes a cup back into the room and spills it in his lap, which makes him yell. I find this amusing.

The next speaker shows a lot of slides. Some are done in nice restful pastel colours, which renders the text unreadable. One is a graph which is supposed to show the dramatic increase in something or other but has been mounted in the carousel back to front, so it shows a dramatic decrease. This causes a little merriment, which makes the speaker cross. As the room is blacked out we can't make notes. The speaker finishes half an hour early and the organiser calls for an impromtu question and answer session. Two questions are asked, neither of which the speaker is able to answer. Apparently he is standing in for someone else who couldn't come but briefed him last night. We break early for lunch.

Lunch is a buffet and there is only one serving point so the service is very slow. Two delegates who are vegetarian are offered omelettes. The food however is excellent and there is a lot of wine, with our glasses constantly being topped up by sharp-eyed waiters.

Over the coffee, one of the afternoon speakers who has drunk too much, starts having a loud argument with the organiser over some lost slides. There is then a most entertaining fight, with delegates placing bets on the outcome. I win £5. The police are called and the event is aborted.

And, the funny thing is, none of us seem to care …

CHAPTER ONE

THE

CONFERENCE

BUSINESS

According to a survey carried out in 1991, the amount of money spent by UK organisations running conferences in the UK was more than £6 billion.

Many organisations have a need for their employees, shareholders or customers to meet for a great many reasons. The occasion might be an Annual General Meeting (AGM), a problem-solving management conference, a dealer or customer event such as a product launch, a seminar or a scientific or academic meeting. The event could be anything from 20 delegates sitting around a boardroom table for a day to a 2 000 delegate event run over a week in a modern convention centre with hundreds of speakers and sessions. Events can be put on by a company, a trade association or a scientific or academic body. They could be for the purpose of announcement, the dissemination of information, motivation, education, interaction, training, selling, making money and any combination of these.

Most events are organised by employees of the organisations staging them, usually as a small part of their total job. (The number of organisations in the UK running enough events to be able to justify a full-time internal person is probably only a few hundred.) Some will do the whole of the job, that is designing the programme, selecting speakers, choosing the venue, negotiating prices and handling all the necessary organisation and administration. Others will just be involved with the organisational and administrative aspects. Some will call upon the services of outside contractors for help.

In terms of a full-time career therefore, the 'industry' offers little. Those jobs that do exist will be with the few organisations that can afford the luxury of a full-time organiser, or with companies specialising in organising events for others. There may also be openings in audiovisual production companies and for specialist conference staff in some of the larger hotels and other conference venues.

This is not to say that a study of the business and the special skills needed to succeed will not be worthwhile. On the contrary, skills in a specialism such as conference organisation can be a significant advantage in the increasingly competitive job market, like being fluent in another language. It is not, however, a 'profession' in any sense of the word. There are very few recognised qualifications in the UK, although a start has been made in assessing the feasibility of an NVQ, and a course in Event Management, which also covers exhibitions, is held at the Fife College of Technology in Kirkcaldy, Scotland (tel. 0592 262414).

Despite this, or perhaps because of it, the organisation of events is something that attracts a lot of people and it is not hard to see why. There is a lot of responsibility, a wide range of talents to be employed and a chance to work closely with people. Good organisers tend to be extrovert, sociable and confident individuals who like nothing better than the challenge of pulling a host of details together to form the perfect event. They love the fun of troubleshooting, of problem-solving and the feeling of satisfaction that comes from coping.

Talking to full-time conference organisers provides some useful insights into the job from the advice given: 'Never take yes for an answer'; 'Always keep a sense of humour'; 'A good organiser is invisible'; and, 'Be like a swan – serene and unruffled above, but paddling frantically underneath.'

For those who want to venture out into the conference industry pond there are a few trends that are worth knowing about.

The recession of the early 90s has wrought some changes, some of which may be permanent. As organisations have cut back their spending on conferences, events have become smaller (with fewer delegates), shorter, with a smaller audiovisual element, and are on a 'more work, less play' basis. More are staged over weekends, using less costly hotels (perhaps the ones without leisure centres), as well as academic venues.

Some organisers are finding bargains overseas, especially in other parts of Europe, and the tendency to consider overseas venues is one which has grown, and will continue to grow with the development of the EC.

Despite the recession, there has been a growing awareness of the financial value of conferences by both buyers and sellers. Sellers of venues have formed various consortia to pool funds and promote jointly. Destinations have formed specialist convention bureaux to target specifically the valuable market, some offering free civic facilities for large residential events. Some buyers have used their commercial buying power to put pressure on venues and destinations to change attitudes and even laws. In particular, the Gay Rights movement has been successful in this respect, arranging and encouraging boycotts of places like Scarborough, which now accepts meetings of homosexuals, and the Isle of Man, where homosexuality is now no longer illegal.

Lastly, there has been an upsurge in technology aimed at replacing the traditional conference. Conferences by telephone and by closed-circuit TV systems, perhaps allowing delegates in different countries the chance to interact with each other, will, if you believe the sales pitch of those selling such systems, 'revolutionise the industry'.

For those who don't believe this, or who don't want to believe it, there is hope and it springs from the fact that the conference business is about people. Apparently, the technology has not enjoyed the impact predicted and this is due to the fact that human beings still want to meet each other face to face; to enjoy good food and drink together; to talk to others of their choice and share confidences privately; to rub shoulders with their peers; and to experience fully the stimulating change of pace, diet and company and perhaps some enjoyable travelling, a good live event can bring. Seeing it on television is one thing; being there is quite another, and this vital difference looks likely to keep traditional conferencing going for a long time to come.

CHAPTER TWO

FINDING A VENUE

A few organisations running conferences and small meetings will be fortunate enough to have their own in-house meeting rooms. Indeed some have even taken to offering such facilities to other planners of events, often at very favourable prices. Or it may be that a conference by telephone, or an in-house teleconference by closed-circuit TV is chosen.

For most, however, the job of finding a suitable venue in which to hold the event will be a primary and fundamental element, and it is this task which is now addressed. A poor or ill-advised choice can ruin the whole programme and bring the organiser's aspirations, not to mention reputation and future job prospects, crashing down.

A start should be made by looking closely at the actual needs of the event in terms of:

- number of delegates meeting
- number and size of meetings rooms needed
- amount of ancillary space needed for registration, an organisers' office, breakout meetings, storage of materials, speakers' 'ready' rooms, beverage breaks, banqueting and maybe for an exhibition area
- number and type of bedrooms needed
- time for which each will be required

- time of year/month/day(s)
- approximate location or city required
- delegate needs
- budget available

A lot of the above will depend on the type of event; the needs of a one-day single session seminar for 200 will clearly be different to those of a five-day residential training course for 50, or those of a three-day conference for 1 000 with a 1 000 square metre exhibition attached. Once the profile of the event is known, some preliminary decisions as to the destination, type of location and type of venue can be made.

Destination and location

The destination is commonly dictated by the delegates and their expectations, especially if they are paying for the event themselves. For many UK trade association members, the right choice for the annual conference may be a coastal resort with good access to shops, restaurants and clubs and a range of local attractions and activities suitable for any visiting family. Organisers of commercial business seminars may find that outside London, Birmingham and Manchester it is hard to get large numbers together. Sales conferences, where company employees may have to travel long distances may be located for the benefit of the majority and held near to motorways, to keep costs of time and travel down. Costs will have a bearing; many organisers arrange nothing in London due to the relatively high price of meeting there. Some deliberately avoid 'tourist traps' such as Cambridge, Edinburgh and York during the Spring to Autumn season, and also exhibition areas such as Birmigham and Harrogate whenever there is a show on, for the same reason of cost. Weather may also play a part in the initial selection process; a venue in a remote location might be perfect in the summer, but less so in midwinter when it might even be cut off by snowfalls. This may be especially applicable to events overseas.

An out-of-town choice may well be cheaper, as well as being easier to get to by car, safer, have better parking facilities, larger rooms and, perhaps most important of all, a management that values the business

The Riviera Centre, Torquay (*Source:* English Riviera Tourist Board)

more than those at some of the more popular city centre venues. On the other hand, the city centre is likely to offer a wider choice of accessible shops, restaurants, clubs, theatres and other attractions as well as good public transport and a larger range of venues from which to choose. For a weekend conference, the price might well be lower than the out-of-town option, and delegates, most of whom will live in the country or suburbs, might prefer the exciting atmosphere of a city centre for a few days.

Resorts offer a relaxing environment away from the hustle and bustle of work and may be the right choice for the longer event with an accent on leisure, especially if partners and sometimes children may attend. There will be a huge range of accommodation in every price range and some good prices 'out of season' especially on weekdays at most venues (see page 28 for another aspect of this). Many resorts will have their own convention centre for larger events. There are various problems associated with resorts such as the distances involved (the better ones being often located away from centres of population), the limited range of local companies supplying ancillary services such as audiovisual facilities, and the mentality of some venue managements, who are more used to serving tourists than business groups. Seaside locations have a special appeal to most however due to the 'holiday' feel they engender.

Airport locations have their advantages for short, strictly business meetings as delegates can fly in and out the same day. Road and rail communications are also usually good (London Heathrow is the exception) and prices can be quite reasonable for their high-quality facilities.

Type of venue

There is a very large choice of venue available, especially for small conferences and meetings and some of the main options are detailed below.

Hotels

Some now specialise in conference business and have built dedicated conference or training suites to serve the market. Most have all-purpose function rooms which may be suitable. Many hotels, particularly the higher grade ones, can offer meeting rooms, banqueting facilities and accommodation for most small and medium-sized events, all under one roof and in an appropriate atmosphere, and these will be the first choice of most organisers.

Convention centres

These offer suitable meeting areas and banqueting for larger events but no accommodation, although this is sometimes available at an on-site but independently-run hotel. Large areas for exhibitions are commonly available. Many serve a public function too, holding concerts and sports events, and fixed seating in a purpose-built auditorium may be available for hire. Some incorporate public facilities, such as a leisure pool. Those organisers looking for a low-cost option for large events, where delegates can be accommodated in modest hotels and guest houses, will probably choose the convention centre.

Universities and colleges

In terms of cost, these generally offer significant advantages. Food is often of a very high quality, meetings rooms are specially designed with a range of audiovisual equipment included, and bedrooms increasingly offer ensuite toilet and bathroom facilities. The atmosphere is obviously an educational one but many delegates enjoy the nostalgic experience of going 'back to school'.

However, for some events, university accommodation, which is only available in holiday periods, may not be convenient, and the bedrooms may be considered to be of guest-house rather than hotel standard making them unsuitable for some business groups. Those universities and colleges that have invested in ensuite refurbishments may be as costly as a three-star hotel, and prices should be carefully checked. Because educational establishments cannot easily let individual rooms like a hotel, the penalties for room reduction in the event of cancellation or postponement will also be higher.

Management training centres
Being dedicated to the business of training, these can offer an attractive package to this specialised market. Prices commonly include dedicated organisers' offices, and audiovisual equipment with on-site operators, along with many other facilities. The cost of extras such as telephone calls, faxes and photocopying will often be far lower than the prices charged by hotels.

Accommodation will generally be similar to that provided by universities and colleges and will be functional, since the accent is on work rather than play. Again the penalty for cancellation will be high.

Theatres
These can generally offer a competitive hire price, a sense of occasion, comfortable seating for larger groups and dedicated audiovisual arrangements.

Banqueting space may be a problem and prices for food and drink are often quite high.

Boats
Conferences afloat are generally those where some kind of novelty or incentive element is needed. The delegates are completely captive, which may be another important factor in choosing this type of venue.

The budget for a cruise ship will need to be generous, and bad weather may be a problem since many operators only look for conference business in the winter season. However, river boats and barges are a useful luxury option for small events at any time of year.

Theme parks and holiday camps

For events where families are included, these are a useful option to consider. Parks abroad have already won a substantial amount of business from conference organisers here, and parks in the UK are slowly becoming more aware of the potential market.

The problem is that, currently in the UK, on-site accommodation, if available at all, is very much of the 'chalet' type, and meetings rooms are usually all-purpose and small. In addition, management is geared to serve the tourist.

Other options

Other structures that can be hired for meetings are public buildings such as museums, art galleries, sports centres and schools. Facilities at football, rugby, cricket and tennis grounds may also be hired, along with those at racecourses. As competition becomes fiercer, exhibition centres and airports that once had 'gentlemen's agreements' not to build conference facilities and compete with hotels, are now doing so successfully. Organisations such as trade unions, associations, clubs, institutes, societies and commercial companies sometimes hire out their in-house facilities too. Some of the more unusual places in which conferences have been held include trains, planes, temporary structures, such as marquees, and even aircraft hangars, converted gasometers, caves and catacombs!

Sources of information

There are a large number of sources of information on venues. Some can be highly recommended and some will need to be treated with scepticism.

Another conference organiser

This is the favoured choice of most in the business. An impartial recommendation from another organiser who has recently used a venue can be extremely valuable. A number of trade associations of conference organisers exist, and the access gained to other specialists and their knowledge, especially for overseas events, can be well worth the joining fee (see Appendix 1 for a list). It is worth noting however, that the independent organiser who runs events for a living (PCO) will not generally share their knowledge or expertise for free.

Convention and visitors' bureaux

Often part of the local tourist board, these exist to distribute information about their area and to recommend venues within it. In terms of useful general information the bureaux can be very helpful, and some may offer a booking service, on which they make a profit. In theory, the bureaux should be impartial, something that many claim to be. In practice, they are not as they are funded by those members (hotels and attractions) who pay for advertising in the various bureaux or tourist board publications. Bureaux will usually only distribute information about those who advertise, and this often excludes some very worthwhile venues for conferences and accommodation, especially at the budget price level.

Directories

Sadly, there are no impartial directories produced for the conference organiser. Most specialist publications are funded by advertising and only list, like the convention bureaux, those who pay.

In fact some of the best sources, for those looking for good quality hotel venues with good food are the independent consumer guides such as the *Egon Ronay Hotel and Restaurant Guide*, the *Michelin Guide*, the guides produced by the AA and RAC organisations and those published by the Consumers' Association such as *The Good Hotel Guide* and *The Good Food Guide*. These however do not publish meetings room data, and it is worth noting that the star ratings awarded by the AA or RAC are a measure of the facilities, not the service or food.

Computer software

There are a handful of venue information systems available on computer disk and these can save time for those planning a number of events.

Trade bodies

Generally these will only distribute information about their members, who pay to belong to the body. Some have drawn up a code of practice and invariably claim that use of their members' venues or services guarantees a high level of service and 'professionalism' for the conference organiser. Such claims should be regarded with caution.

Venue consortia

Some venues have joined various consortia that take on the marketing of the hotel and publish a directory of members. As with paid directories, these are marketing operations and offer little of value to the conference organiser.

Trade magazines

In general, these can be discounted since the majority of editorial is of the 'advertorial' variety published for the benefit of advertisers and potential advertisers, and not for readers (see Appendix 2).

The most used sources

In June 1991, a group of conference organisers were asked to identify their most valued source of venue information.

The results of the survey are shown below:

Source	%
Recommendation from other organiser	38
Personal experience as delegate/guest or on inspection visit	31
Directories	19
Convention/visitors' bureaux	8
Industry trade association	4
Exhibitions	0
Trade magazines	0
Venue consortia	0
	100

Survey source: *The Meetings File* pub'd by The Meetings Forum

While the results may not be what the venues would like to hear, it is interesting and significant that many final choices were not made until the venue had been experienced at first hand.

Our next chapter therefore deals with the important inspection visit, a vital stage in venue selection.

Points for Discussion

1 What factors are likely to affect the success of
   a) a destination and b) a venue, in terms of attracting conferences?
2 What would be the advantages and disadvantages of running a conference in an academic venue?
3 Why have hotels been so successful in winning conference business?
4 Under what circumstances would venues other than hotels or universities be a feasible choice?
5 What would be the most impartial sources of information about destinations and venues? And the least impartial?

CHAPTER THREE

INSPECTION VISITS

Ideally, all initial inspections should be made by the conference organiser incognito, preferably while another meeting is going on. This is so that the venue can be assessed from the viewpoint of a standard guest rather than a hosted VIP (see Chapter Four). There will however, be, some occasions when this is just not possible, and an organised inspection is carried out with the cooperation of the venue or venues short-listed for further examination.

Such inspections are important because there is much that cannot be ascertained from a brochure. The experienced organiser will travel to the venue the way most delegates will, to experience at first hand any problems with finding it or reaching it. Judgements will be made on the overall first impressions, the attitude of the staff, the quality, colours, style and condition of furnishings, the ease of getting from one area to another, and so on. Many experienced organisers make a check-list of points they need to cover which is a good idea. Others carry tape recorders for easy note-taking and even camcorders to improve their recall of specific rooms and areas when a large number have been inspected.

It is sometimes easier to attend one of the group inspection visits organised by hotels, tourist boards, convention bureaux, trade associations and some trade magazines. These give an opportunity, often over a weekend, to inspect a variety of venues within a location in the company of other organisers, an aspect that can be a most valuable opportunity to add to one's own personal network. From the host's point of view, it is more economic to deal with a small group (usually 6–12) rather than with individual buyers, and the friendly atmosphere of these inspections is also beneficial. Details of upcoming inspection visits are usually circulated by direct invitation but one trade association, the Association of Conference Organisers (ACE) organises regular visits for its members, and the meetings industry newsletter *Meetings File* also lists inspection visits (see Appendices 1 and 2).

During the inspection, organisers will probably want to see conference rooms, bedrooms and public areas and we will now consider these separately. As a guide, it generally takes one to two hours to inspect fully a venue, which includes time for asking questions.

The conference room

It is worth remembering that delegates will probably be spending the bulk of the conference actually in the conference room. It therefore follows that the room or rooms used for the business of meeting are as important, if not more so, than the bedroom accommodation, and attention should be paid to the general look, feel and smell of the room as well as the more technical aspects.

Room layout

There are a number of ways to lay out a conference room for delegates and the layout chosen will greatly depend on the type of conference. For short meetings, large numbers, or where cost is a problem, the theatre-style layout is used. Where delegates have to write, the classroom-style layouts are popular. If maximum interaction and discussion is needed then the U-shape or hollow square is appropriate. Other variations are shown opposite.

Space

The venue should be able to tell the organisers the maximum number of delegates that can be accommodated in a given room with a given layout. This figure is usually calculated on a delegate-per-square-metre basis but the number quoted should be treated with caution since several factors can affect it. For instance, an odd-shaped room or one with pillars or other obstructions will mean that some floor space will be lost. Low

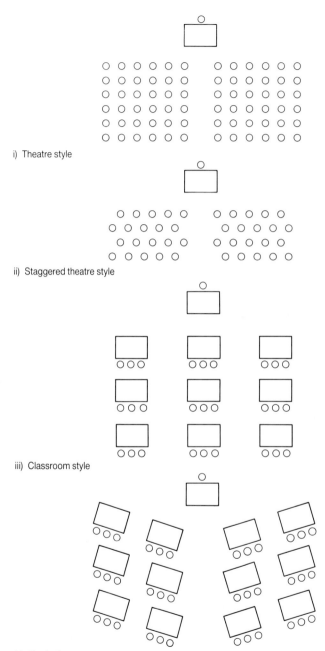

i) Theatre style

ii) Staggered theatre style

iii) Classroom style

iv) Herringbone classroom style

Conference room layouts

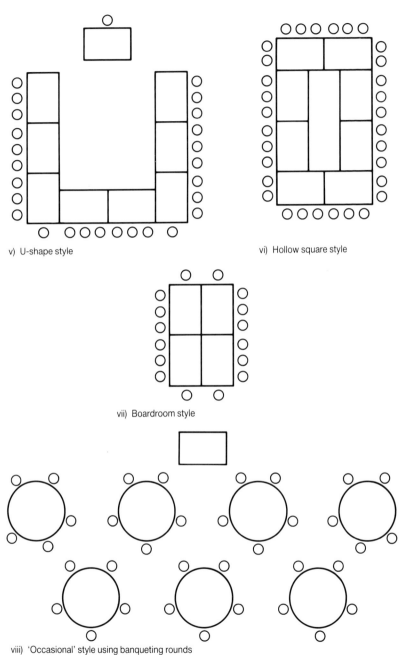

v) U-shape style

vi) Hollow square style

vii) Boardroom style

viii) 'Occasional' style using banqueting rounds

Conference room layouts

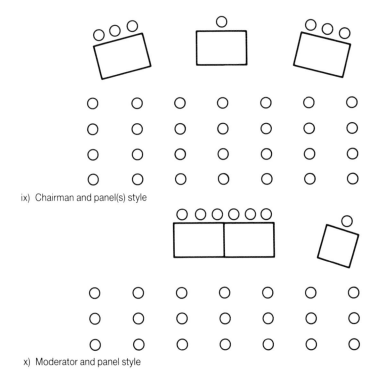

ix) Chairman and panel(s) style

x) Moderator and panel style

Conference room layouts

ceilings may mean that delegates have to sit further apart, or herring-bone style to see the screen. Back projection of slides, films or video will also take up valuable space (see page 88).

In addition to these factors, the venues' own calculations of this figure vary considerably. As a guide, a theatre-style layout will use 1–1.5 m² per delegate. However, one British hotel claims to fit 200 delgates into a 102 m², around half or less than that allowed by most other UK venues! A classroom-style layout usually needs around 3 m² per delegate, depending on the width of tables, and the U-shape or hollow square layout about 4 m². For a reception, around 1 m² per delegate should be allowed. However, the organiser should always check the maximum number of people allowed in a room by the fire regulations. Other factors which could cut down the amount of available space are the registration desk, coffee area, cloakroom, and staging or tables for literature if they are placed in the room.

The audiovisual equipment layout will be affected by the ceiling height, and in a large room holding 500 or more people in a theatre-style layout, it is not unusual for 6–8 m ceiling heights to be insisted upon so that the screen can be high enough off the ground for everyone to see it (see Chapter Eight). Sadly, many hotels claim to have a conference suite when what they really have is a function room, with 3 m high or sloping ceilings, or with chandeliers, which significantly cut the overhead clearance. (Chandeliers may however be retractable, or removable for a fee.) As well as affecting the use of audiovisual equipment, a low ceiling can become oppressive for delegates.

Lighting

Light is something else that affects delegates, and many organisers now insist that conference rooms have some source of natural light to help reduce the 'shut in' feeling. A disadvantage here is that a large picture window with a superb view could be very distracting.

Artificial lighting in a conference room is another important element. Organisers should try to find the controls themselves, unaided and turn the lights on, to check them. Can they easily be dimmed? If the room is partitioned, are there separate lighting controls in each section? Or might you have to go into someone else's meeting to adjust your own lights? Ventilation, heating and air-conditioning should also be assessed, which is a good reason for seeing the room when a meeting is in progress. How long does the system take to be operational? Can it be controlled by the organiser, from the room, or from the partitioned area? Ventilation is important; a meeting room next to a leisure centre may be, understandably perhaps, hot and stuffy and not really suitable for any kind of meeting.

Noise

Noise intrusion can sometimes be the fault of the venue; some conference rooms are too close to restaurants and kitchens. At one conference, at the otherwise excellent Viking Hotel in York, delegates were treated to the chef's lively rendition of *O Sole Mio* as lunch was being prepared. Luckily, his cooking was a lot better than his singing, but the interruption was nevertheless unwelcome. Other noise intrusions can occur when a room has outside walls near a main road or 'soundproof' dividers between areas which are anything but. Problems can also be caused by noisy air-conditioning units and chandeliers that 'clink' when the ventilation system is switched on. Floors should be considered too. A marble or polished wood surface will mean that late arrivals will be clicking their way across it and this could cause a disturbance. Even the type of roof should be assessed; at one UK exhibition venue, the Business Design Centre, a few years ago, a hailstorm on a tin roof was so noisy that it drowned out the speaker. Doors, especially those used as a delegates' exit whilst the event is going on, should be checked to ensure that they do not creak.

Other factors

Mirrors also have an impact on the use of the room as they can reflect the light into delegates' or speakers' eyes, and allow the audience to see around the back of a back-projection set. Most importantly, the natural acoustics of the room should be considered before AV requirements can be determined. Some rooms are 'dead', which can be demonstrated by clapping the hands together and listening for any echo. However, the presence of an audience will alter the acoustics and rooms with balconies can be especially troublesome in this regard. In addition, the shape and size of a room, its ceiling height and surfaces on the walls, floor and ceiling will all affect a room's natural acoustic qualities.

Equipment

In terms of equipment it is worth reviewing and inspecting what the venue provides. Will the equipment include staging, lecterns, basic audiovisual items, coat rails and wastepaper bins? With table layouts are pads, pencils, blotters, sweets, cordials, mineral water and jugs of iced-water all supplied? Are the table coverings which are used the dark-coloured felt type or the standard white table linen used in the restaurant? Are the chairs comfortable? Some organisers may need to check for special equipment and features such as projection rooms, fixed screens, simultaneous interpretation facilities (often wrongly termed 'simultaneous translation') and special training facilities such as wall surfaces to pin or stick things to, built-in video facilities, closed-circuit TV and observation rooms.

Safety

Finally, organisers should always note the fire safety provisions. There should be two exits from the room with clear and lit EXIT signs above

A well-equipped conference room (*Source*: Hilton UK)

the doors. Organisers should walk through fire exit doors, along fire exit routes and to the outside of the building to check that the route is well lit, with no obstructions such as stored furniture, and that all fire doors can be opened from the inside.

Bedrooms

After the meeting room, the bedroom is the other area that delegates will spend a lot of time in and this should be suitable for the purpose and objectives of the event.

There may well be variations between 'standard singles', 'executive singles' and 'de luxe', and the details of these should be checked. The differences could relate to the room size, bed size, bathroom size, view from the window, and the facilities provided. It may be a matter of just a handful of extra toiletries and a different colour scheme. Organisers should find out how many rooms there are in each category and whether the 'superior' categories are available for delegates on the day. The availability of suites for VIPs should be explored, as should the existence

A suite bedroom at the Brighton Metropole (*Source*: Brighton Metropole)

A standard room at the Brighton Metropole (*Source*: Brighton Metropole)

of 'no smoking' rooms. Organisers should note the overall room size of bedrooms, the size of the bed, how comfortable it is and the overall condition and cleanliness of the fixtures and furnishings. A good place to check the hotel's commitment to cleanliness is the top of the bathroom door frame, and finger run along this may reveal a failing in this general area.

If delegates are going to work in their bedrooms then there will need to be an adequate writing surface and, something that is often missed, adequate lighting to read and write by. There should be ample closet space and hangers, and drawer space too, if the event is a long residential one. There should also be tea and coffee facilities; delegates waiting to get to sessions should not have to wait for room service. A television is usually regarded as an essential; even at events where the accent is heavily on work, many people like to watch, or at least listen to, the breakfast news programme.

The bathroom area is very important. The bath should be large enough to actually take a bath in – not always the case with the more modern facilities – and there should also be a shower. Plenty of bath towels should be provided and the toiletries should at least include soap, shampoo, and bath/shower gel. Other items that might be supplied, and are often welcome, are shower caps, body lotion, aftershave, cotton-wool balls, shoe shine kits and sewing kits. The bathroom should be well lit, especially around the mirror area. Other facilities that may be provided, and that some consider essential, are hair-driers, irons, ironing boards, trouser presses, full-length mirrors, direct-dial telephones, non-allergic pillows, bathrobes, fridges and mini-bars.

From a safety aspect, all rooms should have a notice giving clear information on what to do in case of fire, with two exit routes clearly shown. Smoke detectors are highly desirable and guests should be able to open the windows. For security purposes there should be a spyhole in the door and a safety-chain. Some venues supply small safes in the room for valuables.

Some luxury items which are becoming more common in hotel rooms include satellite TV receivers and video players. This last item may not just be for entertainment; one hotel group, Forte, have installed video players in special 'organisers' bedrooms' which can be used for review of videos played during the conference. At the Smoke House Hotel,

Mildenhall, there are video players in every room and these have proved useful in training sessions where delegates efforts are videoed and can then be viewed in the comfort and privacy of their own hotel room.

Public areas

Organisers should note the suitability of public areas for the event. Will the parking area be large enough for all the vehicles that will arrive? Is the reception area large enough for when the delegates check in? Is there a shop, and does it sell basics such as toothpaste, razors, basic toiletries, headache and indigestion tablets, cough and cold remedies, plasters, newspapers and magazines? Are there enough lifts of sufficient size to move all the delegates down to sessions without unreasonable delays? Are there enough public toilets?

It is also a good idea to walk through the areas between meeting rooms and banqueting halls. Is it a long or complicated hike? Are the signs clear enough for someone in the venue for the first time?

More concern is now being shown for disabled people and a check with the venue will reveal the management's attitude and commitment to this aspect. The main criteria for those in a wheelchair travelling independently, as listed by the Holiday Care Service are:

- parking or drop off points at main entrance
- permanent ramps (1:12) or level access throughout
- all doors in public areas and bedrooms more than 750 mm wide
- handrails by toilet and bath
- toilet and bath height between 45 and 50 cm
- lifts to have minimum clear door opening of 750 mm and an internal space of at least 1200 x 800 mm
- in all areas used by guests there must be unobstructed space of at least 1100 x 700 mm per person

Interestingly, at the time of writing, only two central London hotels, the Copthorne Tara and the Ibis at Euston, comply with the above.

In the USA, a relatively new act, the Americans with Disabilities Act, stipulates a number of facilities that must now be provided for disabled people.

Other considerations

There are a number of other aspects that organisers may want to check whilst in the venue. These may include:

- the check-in and check-out times

- the policies on payment or prepayment terms

- details of any planned venue refurbishments or construction nearby which might affect the event

- details of any other meetings being held in the venue at the same time, if known (noise levels might be a problem, or the organisation holding the event might be a competitor)

- details of restaurant space available; the venue may have meetings space for 300 but restaurant space for only 150

The inspection visit is an essential and time-consuming part of venue selection and evaluation. A good organiser will plan to use the time as effectively as possible to make a careful and detailed evaluation of all the venue elements necessary for a successful event.

Points for Discussion

1 What are the pros and cons of carrying out an inspection visit incognito?
2 Is it ethical to accept free hospitality from a number of venues when only one will be chosen?
3 List the aspects of the venue that can only be evaluated by an inspection visit.
4 What would be an ideal conference room, and why?
5 What would you look for when inspecting a hotel bedroom?

CHAPTER FOUR

NEGOTIATION

In a perfect world there would, of course, be no need for negotiation. Prices charged by all vendors would be entirely reasonable and buyers with unlimited budgets would pay them, plus a tip for good service.

Life is, happily perhaps, nothing like that, and there is sufficient difference between the first prices offered by venues and the final prices agreed by conference organisers to challenge the negotiation skills of even the most hardened and experienced haggler.

Negotiating a good deal really is quite fulfilling. There is probably nothing so satisfying as, having sat through a tough negotiating session, coming away with a final package with which both parties are happy: the win/win situation described in textbooks on the subject.

The win/win is certainly a considerable improvement on the win/lose outcome, which usually turns into a lose/lose situation as the injured party claws back some advantage or other. A true story will illustrate this.

A few years ago, a conference organiser negotiated a particularly low price for a one-day seminar package with a hotel in West London. Included in the eight-hour rate was morning coffee and afternoon tea. At the mid-morning break the organiser received a number of complaints from delegates who, having paid several hundred pounds to attend, were angry that there were no biscuits and criticised him for his meanness. When the organiser queried this with the banqueting manager he was told, with only a slight smirk, 'But you didn't order biscuits, sir'. During the afternoon, one of the hottest on record, the air-conditioning in the conference suite failed. A number of delegates actually fainted and one was taken to hospital. The organiser insisted that the room-hire portion of the bill, around £2 000, was knocked off. After an argument, the hotel agreed, a saving which paid for a lot of biscuits! The next time the organiser came to negotiate with the hotel they had some rather special prices to discuss...

Perhaps, as one trainer in negotiation skills (John Winkler) puts it, it's all just a game, and one to be enjoyed. Certainly in countries where haggling is expected, and welcomed, no one seems to take any of the cut and thrust too seriously or personally, and this attitude should, the author feels, be encouraged in the UK. The more good natured the process is, the more mutually advantageous the relationship will be between the two parties. This chapter is therefore about playing the game better.

Know the value of the event

It is obviously vital to assess how much an event is worth, not just to the venue, but to the surrounding community. A large 'captive audience' of delegates can have quite an impact on the local economy during their stay. This factor means that an event is valuable to the area in which it takes place, and some conference organisers are successful in negotiating free conference rooms at the civic centre on the basis that their event will be filling local hotels and restaurants. Also negotiable with convention bureaux and local authorities are free civic receptions, transportation, sightseeing tours, welcome signs, and staff. Useful materials (town guides, transparencies for OHPs) are commonly offered and press contacts supplied by the bureau can be especially helpful.

When talking terms with hotels, it is worth bearing in mind that there are few so perishable commodities in the world as unsold airline seats, unsold exhibition space and unsold hotel rooms, both the meeting-in and the sleeping-in varieties. It is also worth knowing that the average cost of servicing a hotel bedroom in the UK is less than £10, so that anything gained by the hotel over this figure makes a welcome contribution to fixed and other running costs. In general, hotels make a profit of 60 per cent on bedrooms and 30 per cent on food and beverages, so they are more likely to cut prices on rooms than on banqueting.

The size and type of event may also have a bearing on its value to the hotel, and not always in an obvious way. Surprisingly, an event that needs every hotel room in town might not be in a great negotiating position, and a hotel with 500 bedrooms and 10 meetings rooms might well charge an especially high price for a conference which took eight of its meetings rooms and only 100 bedrooms. Having only two meeting rooms spare might mean they have to turn away another conference needing five meeting rooms. A conference occupying only one meeting room but 250 bedrooms could be most attractive.

Organisers of residential conferences will often look for hotels they can completely fill on the assumption that the hotel staff will give the delegates their undivided attention. This may be true, but conference organisers could be paying a very high price for this facility. A hotel with only 100 bedrooms faced with filling them all for an event is unlikely to discount much since such discounts will have a maximum impact on the total gross profit for the period. A 500-bed hotel, on the other hand, can take a view that 100 of its rooms could be discounted, especially if booked early, as long as the other 400 were sold at near to full price. By the same token, a late booking could also work if the hotel had already sold 400 of its 500 rooms at close to full price.

Certain types of delegates may be more profitable to a venue than others. For example, teetotallers who like to eat healthily and swim 100 lengths of the pool every day are unlikely to swell the hotel's profits as much as big eaters who order aperitifs, wine, liqueurs and cigars with their meals and who like nothing better than drinking single malt scotches in the hotel bar until the early hours.

Another factor which could bring the price down is that if the event has a well-known personality speaking, the venue might wish to capitalise on their appearance in its public relations activities.

Other events which might have more appeal for a venue are those where a high proportion of delegates bring partners and share a room, and also events where delegates are encouraged to arrive before the conference and stay on for a few days afterwards.

Know the market

There are certain times when hotels may be rather more open to offers than others. In general, hotels in city centres will be full from Monday to Thursday with business customers (though meetings rooms may be empty) and less busy at the weekend, especially on Friday night. Resort hotels and country house hotels may well be full over the weekend and empty from Monday to Thursday. In terms of seasonal trends, most four- and five-star hotels in UK resorts such as Brighton and Bournemouth are anxious to fill their empty bedrooms in July and August whilst all the three-star, two-star and one-star hotels and guest houses may be full. This is because most UK holidaymakers with enough money for a four- or five-star hotel would rather go overseas in the summer, to guarantee getting good weather. By September, the position is reversed as the better quality hotels start to fill up with conferences.

There may also be some other factors affecting availability. Hotels in London tend to fill up for Wimbledon fortnight and those in Birmingham are well-known for going into something of a frenzy when a big exhibiton is running at the local National Exhibition Centre.

Something else to be aware of is that exhibitions staged with conferences are not generally liked by hotels, for good reason. The presence of exhibition stands in a large suite may mean that the room cannot be used for a profitable evening banqueting function and the organiser will be charged accordingly, the price often hidden in the total price for the conference. An allowance for damage to the hotel suite may also be a factor in the price. Organisers running exhibitions alongside their conferences to raise revenue, need to establish precisely how much better a price they could negotiate without the exhibition, an important part of the real cost.

Know the vendor

The above comments regarding exhibition space do not generally apply to convention centres where the exhibition space is dedicated as such, and where the centre does not usually run evening banquets. A knowledge of the vendor is, clearly, useful, and as much information as possible should be obtained before any approach is made. Some of the basic information to be gained can be found in Chapter Two on venue sourcing.

It may be possible however to discover what kind of price might be offered *before* making initial contact. Other conference organisers can be a most useful source in this regard and the prudent operator will not miss any opportunity to build up a network of people to call. Often the venue will supply names of customers although these are likely to be satisfied ones who paid the full rate.

Another useful source of pricing information can be the short-break brochures published by tour operators offering accommodation-only packages at selected hotels. Tour operators negotiate some of the lowest prices around and the offers made to the general public are often lower than the prices for accommodation charged to higher-spending delegates brought in by conference organisers. This is invariably because the hotel knows the delegates are something of a captive market and sets its prices accordingly. If conference organisers take the price charged in the brochures and deduct 30 per cent, this final price will be close to the price charged to the tour operator, and probably close to the lowest price at which the hotel is prepared to trade, a most useful figure to have in mind when negotiating.

Other specific negotiation opportunities open up when the hotel is a new one and has to carve out quickly its share of the market; prices will often start low to get the business and rise as the hotel sales staff are successful. A hotel that is part of a group may also be receptive to suggestions that other hotels in the group will be receiving conferences run in different areas of the country.

Know the business

Most hotels offer two types of standard rate: an eight-hour and a 24-hour delegate rate. These are expressed as a fixed price per delegate, and represent an alternative to booking meetings rooms, bedrooms and food and beverages on an individual basis.

The eight-hour inclusive delegate rate will include the use of a conference room between 9.00 a.m. and 5.00 p.m., coffee for the delegates on arrival, morning coffee, a lunch and afternoon tea. It may also include the use of some basic audiovisual equipment such as flip charts, an OHP and a video player and monitor. The 24-hour delegate rate will include all this plus accommodation, breakfast and dinner for the delegates.

A Goldenrail short-break brochure (*Source*: Goldenrail Short Breaks and Holidays)

It is worth, however, costing out the exact price to be paid if you agree to the delegate rate as opposed to purchasing the various components separately. As an example, one London hotel was recently quoting an eight-hour delegate rate of £38. This was fine for up to around 50 delegates. At 60 delegates however, it was definitely cheaper to buy the individual components. Teas/coffees were £2.10 each, lunch was £15 and the conference room was £600. The figures worked out thus:

Buying separately

Room	£600.00
Tea/coffee £2.10 x 3 x 60 delegates	£378.00
Lunch £15 x 60 delegates	£900.00
	£1 878.00

Eight-hour delegate rate

60 delegates x £38	£2 280.00

When the 24-hour delegate rates are calculated a similar pattern emerges. Remember that such rates represent the *highest* price that the hotel charges, not the final negotiated rate. In many cases, calculations will reveal that the delegate rate is uncompetitive at a far lower figure than 60 delegates.

An important part of buyer knowledge is the inspection visit (see Chapter Three for more information on these). Many inexperienced organisers will simply call up the sales manager of the hotel and arrange a complimentary lunch, diner or overnight stay, but is this the best option? Probably not.

Is there really any point in simply experiencing the doubtless VIP welcome given to all bringers of business when it is not the package that delegates will get? Will they get the flowers and fruit in the room? The king-sized bed? The spa bath? The instant connection with reception the moment they pick up the telephone? To put a hotel through its paces, it is a better idea to check in incognito, or get someone else to do it, and see the operation through the eyes of a normal guest. Many such visits have had conference organisers quietly leaving the hotel first thing in the morning vowing never to return.

At one modern hotel in Birmingham, the rooms were extremely small and wedge shaped owing to the hotel's circular construction. A casual question to the housekeeping staff, 'Do guests ever comment on the size of rooms here?', brought the response, 'Oh yes, we get complaints every day. Lots of people only stay here once – many get their companies to book them in somewhere else.' Opportunities to talk to such useful sources of information before meeting other staff should be taken.

If no failings are found on the incognito visit, or if they are minor, then an 'official' visit can be arranged, usually with someone handling sales for the venue. Prudent organisers however will still arrive an hour or two early for such appointments and take a look around by themselves. The author recalls waiting by the reception of one well-known conference hotel in Birmingham as a guest approached with an enquiry about the next train to London. She was told, 'You can phone the station from your room', a far cry from 'I'll find out for you'. Little things like this can betray a lot about the general attitude of the venue staff to customers.

The negotiations

Having discovered as much as possible about the venue before meeting the sales staff, it is worth considering the strategy to be adopted at such a meeting. Sales staff at venues are often maligned by organisers who see them as unnecessary and relatively useless individuals whose only objective is to sell and, having obtained the order, just want to move quickly on to the next potential piece of business. Whilst there may be a degree of truth in this, there is no doubt that as far as the negotiation process is concerned, this transient aspect can turn the sales staff into the organiser's greatest allies. Most have to sell in order to live and will often be able to argue a case for discounts and other benefits with their general manager far more forcibly, effectively and with more inside knowledge of the operation than the conference organiser. It is therefore important that the organiser first gains the respect, trust and support of all the sales staff and, with this in mind, we will now go on to look at some negotiator's ground rules.

Prepare
Regard the negotiation process as a two-way sell. The staff at the venue want to sell it, and you want to sell your event to them: its advantages, its

prestige, its potential for profit and the (sadly) low price you have to reach in order to be able to make an agreement. Make a list, therefore, of all the selling points: know the prices charged by the venue to others: know the prices charged by other venues in the area (the local tourist board or convention bureau can be helpful in this respect).

Be nice

A common myth is that good negotiators fold their arms across their chests and grunt as sellers turn cartwheels to please them. This is counter-productive behaviour. If the sales staff like the buyer and sense a desire to reach agreement then they will do more. Sales staff are human beings too and few will put themselves out for someone who is surly.

But gain respect

Respect will be gained as the buyer reveals a knowledge of the business. Showing that the venue's discounted prices to its largest customers are known is one obvious way. Asking intelligent questions is another. If the bedrooms contain no irons, hairdriers, trouser presses, full-length mirrors or tea and coffee-making facilities, ask why. Ask for a list of differences between 'basic' rooms and 'executive' ones. Ask how many are available in each category. Ask about cloakroom arrangements for a day conference. Ask about arrangements for getting messages to delegates, about the operation of a cash bar and about the number of serving points allotted for a buffet. Run a finger along the tops of door sills, and check that windows open.

Don't lie

Don't lie about anything. Once you are found out, word goes round the conference world very quickly and trust is lost.

Be flexible

Never give the impression that only one date, day of the week or month of the year is under consideration. This makes a buyer vulnerable.

Never reveal deadlines

This is another sure way to pay more.

Always talk low prices

Sellers have an inbuilt advantage in that the prices they would like to achieve are published and we all have an overdeveloped and illogical awe and respect of the printed word. To counter the seller's advantage, the buyer must ensure that much lower prices are dropped into the conversation as often as possible, to lower the seller's expectation. Remember that sellers generally set their charges on the basis of what other sellers charge. Buyers should set theirs on the basis of what other buyers actually pay. Venues also commonly charge more to groups they know can pay more, such as insurance and motor companies.

It is also worth remembering that the statement, 'We do not negotiate' means, 'It's negotiable', and, 'We definitely do not negotiate' means, 'It's definitely negotiable'! The claim, 'It's not our policy' means, 'We'll change it, if the price is right'.

Name drop

Always mention names of large, well-known organisers who place lots of business with the venue since they will have probably negotiated the lowest rates. This serves to lower the price expectation gently, to the buyer's advantage.

Always mention the hotel's main competitors. In negotiations, nearly all concessions are made because of the presence of competitive offerings elsewhere. However, do remember that hoteliers talk to each other and will be comparing notes with each other after you have left.

Hint at other business

Perhaps the conference in question will be an annual one looking for a permanent home? Perhaps other conferences, not related, are currently in the planning stage? Perhaps other departments or divisions of the buyer's organisation would be useful sales contacts for the hotel?

Divide to conquer

If relevant, it might be a good idea to divide the event into three main buying areas: meeting rooms, accommodation and ancillary banqueting, and then to get separate quotes. This works especially well when there are a lot of hotels grouped together, perhaps near a convention centre, and it is perfectly feasible that accommodation could be in one hotel, meetings in another and evening meals in a third. Hotels capable of accommodating all three will fight very hard to win all three and will often price accordingly.

Be patient
Be prepared to walk away from a negotiation, to take time to consider an offer made. Prevarication invariably aids the buyer and unsettles the seller.

Disclaim responsibility
A useful ploy is to stress that the decision will be made by someone else, someone who only looks at the lowest price or most attractive offer. Thus such statements as, 'I'll put your offer forward but I don't hold out much hope' or, 'They'll never go for it' can be made in perfect safety.

Look for non-cash aspects
Sellers will often, due to company policy perhaps, be able to include extras far more easily than allowing a price reduction. Experienced conference organisers are aware of all the possibilities and explore them.

- **Free items** Many organisers who put substantial numbers of delegates into a hotel are able to negotiate free meetings room hire, rental of AV equipment, parking, cloakrooms, rooms for speakers and staff meals (often hotels will give one room free for every 50 booked) and events such as hosted cocktail parties. The charging of double rooms at the same price as singles can also be valuable.

- **Cut price items** Special prices can be obtained on meals for staff and speakers; efforts should be made to have such personnel excluded from the normal rate charged for paying delegates.

- **Enhancement** Special treatment, such as room upgrades, VIP service, use of courtesy cars and coaches and use of suites and specially designed conference organisers' rooms are all worth consideration. Some hotels supply a special organiser's office and can offer a dedicated hotel contact for the organiser, two aspects that can make life considerably easier.

Don't underestimate sellers

With reference to all the advice given above it is worth remembering that many sellers are trained in negotiating techniques and, in some cases, will be well aware that they are being manipulated. Indeed it is fair to say that, like in any other sport, a fairly matched pair of players can gain a great deal of enjoyment from the contest. Some tricks used by sellers are clearly worth knowing, and one of the richest sources of information on the subject is a book *Hotel and Catering Sales*, written by expert Derek Taylor which advises hoteliers:

1 Pump the client for other business that might be placed.

2 Stand client in a corner of a room to make it look larger, in the middle to make it look smaller.

3 With an ignorant client who doesn't know much about wine pretend that you are equally ignorant. A claim, 'I couldnt tell a claret from a burgundy' will put them at their ease.

4 Flatter the client; warn staff of their arrival and get them to use the client's name. Warn the telephonist to give especially fast service. When the client visits, meet them at door, make notes, ask intelligent probing questions about the client's aims and objectives. Find out the client's favourite drink and have it put in the room.

Points for Discussion

1 You are planning a three-day event for 200 people at a four-star hotel. What might this be worth in total money to the venue? In non-financial terms?

2 What helpful negotiating information can you discover before making contact with a venue?

3 A venue charges £36 per delegate, at an eight-hour rate. Alternatively the room can be hired for £500, lunch bought for £15.50 and teas/coffee for £2.25. Calculate the best way of buying for 30, 60, 100, 150 and 200 delegates. What is the break even number where prices will be more or less identical?

4 Do liars make good negotiators? What type of person makes the best negotiator?

5 List all the non-cash benefits you could ask a venue for.

THE

AUDIENCE

It is for the benefit of the audience that the majority of events will be staged and it is the audience, whether they are called delegates, participants or attendees, whose needs should be paramount. This is fundamental. At one conference on incentive travel held in Malta and attended by the author it was clear, after a few hours, that the event was being held mainly to give local politicians and local suppliers of services a chance to sell themselves to the audience. A number of delegates, bored by this, did not return after lunch.

Such unhappy occasions are fortunately rare, and most conference organisers will ensure that the content of their programmes is as interesting and relevant to the audience as it can be. Thought should also be given to the social needs of the delegates as well as the impact of the accommodation arrangements, the meetings room (see Chapter Three) and the food and beverages served (see Chapter Seven).

Programming

The objective of the event will dictate the programme created. In the example given above, a three-hour session was run without a break. This may have been because the organisers were concerned that, given the nature of the material, it would be difficult to get bored delegates back in once they had left. As a general rule, a maximum of one and half hours without a break is acceptable since delegates need exercise, or may need simply to go to the toilet. Within the one and half hours it is also a good idea to present the programme as three half-hour segments, to maximise interest and attention.

These segments could be used by three different speakers, perhaps each speaking for 20 minutes and then taking 10 minutes of questions. The segments could also be used to present the material in three different ways using such methods of presentation as a video, a film, a slide show, a panel session, an interview, a staged playlet, an interactive session of audience questions and comment, or a management 'game', these last two being suitable for much longer sessions if desired.

Conference speaker using slides to illustrate his speech (*Source*: ICC Birmingham)

It is worth remembering that delegates will be able to absorb and retain much of the material presented between 10.00 a.m. and 1.00 p.m. After lunch, however, the capacity to do so will decrease, and some wise organisers arrange a maximum of one hour of material, without a break, for the afternoon session. Others, mindful of the stimulation that can be created by interactive and group exercise sessions called ('breakout' or 'syndicate' sessions, where small groups discuss issues which are related to that morning's sessions, for instance), schedule these for after lunch. Some save their most powerful or controversial speaker for the immediate post-lunch 'graveyard' session, when it has been suggested that a delegate's productivity can drop by up to 60 per cent.

If the material presented is especially stimulating and thought-provoking, delegates will wish to discuss the issues raised with each other. Longer coffee breaks, of 45 minutes perhaps, can give them this opportunity.

The need to network with each other is a vital part of events, from the delegates' point of view. Few however, in the UK, are good at circulating; casually engaging in and detaching from conversations as American attendees seem to do so easily, is not a commonly-held skill. There are a number of ways the UK organiser can overcome delegates' natural reticence to mix, and these will include informal social events, such as a welcome buffet to start the conference, exercises and group discussions which mix different combinations of delegates, and 'table topic' sessions which immediately follow a lunch and allow delegates with a common interest in the subject discussed to mix. At one UK one-day business event, the organiser had delegates at the lunch enjoying their starters on one table, their main course on another and their desserts and coffee on another, to encourage networking.

The timing of activities should also be carefully considered in relation to the delegates' needs. A 10.30 a.m. start could allow those travelling long distances time to get to the event without an expensive overnight stay. A finishing time of 4.00 p.m., rather than 5.00 p.m. might be equally acceptable, for similar reasons.

Time simply to relax and switch off is also important in residential programmes, and as a general rule, one and a half or two hours between the end of the daytime sessions and the start of the evening programme is about right. In this time delegates can phone home, take a refreshing walk, swim or run or simply languish in a hot bath and reflect on the state of the world, before enjoying a leisurely dinner.

On the other hand, some successful events work delegates hard, incorporating evening work and even breakfast activities. At one American event, delegates were told to order breakfast in their rooms for 8.00 a.m. and to tune into a closed-circuit channel on the hotel TV to watch a video of the company chairman. This 'Breakfast with the chairman' session was reportedly popular with delegates, although it may seem slightly over the top from a British perspective. One enterprising seller of business videos at another American conference arranged to have previews of his product screened on the bedroom TVs at a pre-arranged time.

Finally, it is worth using a chairman to oversee the smooth running of the event's programme. A good chairman will introduce the subjects and the speakers, keep the speakers to time, and will generate questions at question time. Some will also be able to run a panel session or a moderated forum in which they can take the delegates' point of view and question panellists accordingly.

Sample Programme

0900 – 0930   Coffee and Danish

0930 – 1000   Session 1 – Speaker

1000 – 1030   Session 2 – Speaker

1030 – 1100   Session 3 – Panel session

1100 – 1130   Coffee

1130 – 1200   Session 4 – Video

1200 – 1230   Session 5 – Speaker

1230 – 1300   Session 6 – Interview

1300 – 1345   Lunch

1345 – 1430   Table topics (at lunch tables)

1430 – 1500   Session 7 – Speaker

1500 – 1530   Afternoon tea

1530 – 1600   Session 8 – Speaker

1600 – 1630   Session 9 – Syndicate exercise

1630 – 1700   Session 10 – Questions and conclusions

1700 – 1900   Free time

1900 – 2000   Reception

2000 – 2200   Dinner

Pre-event activity

Most of the work that is done prior to the event tends to be focused on the venue, the audiovisual needs and the banqueting arrangements and it is easy to forget the delegates when handling all the other aspects. If the event is residential then accommodation arrangements will, of course, need to be made, either by booking a block of suitable rooms or by setting up a booking system for delegates' individual requirements (see Chapter Nine).

In the pre-event planning stage there are other aspects which will need attention if things are to run smoothly. At the most basic level, delegates need information about the venue including a good map showing how to get there by train as well as by car. A large number of the little maps found in hotel leaflets are inadequate, especially if the delgates will be arriving in darkness, and it is worth having a very clear, enlarged version drawn with the venue address and telephone number featured boldly. Those travelling by public transport will need to have additional information regarding rail, coach, bus and taxi services and perhaps the name of the nearest underground station. At some large events, where delegates might fly in, courtesy buses are sometimes provided from airports and such arrangements need to be publicised among the delegates.

Many delegates will be leaving a partner or family behind and an information sheet with details of the venue and contact telephone numbers that can be left at home will be much appreciated. Those delegates bringing partners or children will need to know about any special 'partner programmes' or other arrangements made for them.

Delegates will need to be notified of any social events planned for residential conferences, particularly if special dress will be needed, such as formal wear or fancy dress. In some cases this can be hired by delegates from a local retailer or costumier and thought will need to be given to a simple advance order system for this. In general, delegates will feel happier with a dress code laid down by the organiser for the various parts of event, such as 'lounge suits', 'smart casual' or 'casual'. Another important element of pre-event planning which affects the delegates is the need for them to notify the organiser of any dietary requirements, disabilities or medical conditions needing special consideration and the wise organiser will ensure that there is a system for capturing such essential information.

Finally, there are those events, such as the commercial conference, where the organiser knows little about the delegates coming, and so may wish to circulate a form that feeds back information about the delegates, their reasons for attending, and their expectations. Such information is invaluable in fine-tuning the material to fit the audience and may even be incorporated into the opening remarks, to focus attention sharply on the objectives of the event. At one large educational event, the organiser gained some fascinating insights about delegates' opinions on key issues before the conference started by circulating a form, which in itself was a piece of highly relevant and original research. The results were revealed throughout the event and considerably enhanced the value of it in the eyes of the delegates. There could be a useful place for such an exercise at many events, both commercial and in-house.

Considerations at the event

A good organiser will consider the safety, comfort and well-being of delegates whilst at the event.

Safety

It is becoming more common for organisers to consider what they would do in the case of a life-threatening emergency such as a fire. Some safety aspects may be covered by the venue, which may have well-thought-out procedures for evacuation and these should be checked. Ultimately, however, the responsibility for getting delegates out in the event of a fire whilst the conference is taking place should be firmly shouldered by the organiser.

In fact, it can only make good sense to ensure that every delegate knows what to do if the fire alarm goes off and the building has to be evacuated. Many will be in the venue for the first time and will not be familiar with the layout, particularly with regard to where the fire exits are. In one fire in an American hotel, six delegates died when they simply took a wrong turning. It is therefore sound practice to make a short announcement at the start of the event advising delegates:

1 What the fire alarm sounds like (bell, siren, spoken message).

2 Where the fire exits from the conference room are located, and the routes out of the venue.

3 To leave everything behind when evacuating the room.

4 To use emergency stairs, *not* lifts, which will be subject to a power cut in a fire.

5 To walk, not panic and run.

6 Where to meet outside.

It is sad to have to note at this point that many influential sectors of the British conference industry have been less than enthusiastic about making safety announcements. At the 1991 launch of the state-of-the-art International Convention Centre (ICC) in Birmingham, no safety announcement was made to the 500 conference organisers gathered for the occasion, and at an educational conference for conference organisers staged by Forte PLC at their Grosvenor House Hotel, London, in 1990, the independent organiser of the event was not allowed to make a safety announcement on the grounds that it, 'might alarm the guests'. The conference trade press has been noticeably reticent about reporting on the issue, apparently because it cannot be made into a feature around which advertising can be sold, another sad reflection.

Certain other possible emergencies will need to be thought through by the organiser as well. Such things as the possibility of politically-motivated terrorist attacks and the possibility of physical attacks on delegates if the subject is potentially sensitive, such as laboratory experimentation on live animals, will need to be considered. Also ever present is the possibility of medical emergencies such as diabetic coma, epilepsy and cardiac arrest, and some organisers, mindful of these possibilities, are taking training in first aid. Food poisoning is another nightmare for many, and contingency plans, which should include freezing a sample of all meals for analysis, should be laid down with the hotel.

Comfort
There has been a welcome step forward in the conference industry recently with the realisation that hotel banqueting chairs are designed to be sat on for an hour or two at most, not for a whole day, and that once delegates get sore bottoms their ability or inclination to absorb what is presented to them declines considerably with each painful passing hour. Another point to consider is that chairs with arms are much more comfortable, especially when the layout is theatre style and delegates

have no table or desk on which to rest their elbows. Progress has been made in this area and for longer meetings it is now more common to be offered well-padded chairs with arms at the better venues; one hotel chain, Hilton, has satisfied this need with a £300 rocking and swivelling 'executive' chair designed to be used for eight hours or more.

A comfortable, modern executive chair: the Hilton 8-Hour Chair (*Source*: Hilton UK)

The spacing of chairs and room layout is also important: a very closely-spaced 'theatre' layout will discourage audience interaction and participation; an open, U-shape layout, where each delegate can see all the others will encourage it. Delegates will also feel more comfortable and 'protected' with a table in front of them and the U-shape, square, 'classroom' or 'boardroom' styles will provide a surface to write on (see Chapter Three). If a theatre-style layout has to be adopted and delegates need to write, chairs with arms can be adapted for this purpose with clip-on tables, or failing this, delegates can be issued with clipboards. One enterprising organiser gives delegates a box file which is used to carry conference information and can be used as a temporary laptop writing surface.

Lighting, temperature and air circulation in the conference room are important aspects of comfort to consider. Many presenters will virtually black out a room when showing slides, videos, films or overhead transparencies to increase the impact of their images. This can make it impossible for delegates to take notes, should they wish to, and a compromise will need to be found. Dimming the lights to show a film or slides during the 'graveyard session' after lunch is generally accepted to be the best way to send an audience to sleep. A room that is too hot or has poor ventilation will have a similar effect. Remember that the presence of delegates in a room, especially if the layout is theatre style, will have an effect on the temperature and the air, and that heating and air-conditioning systems will take some time to have any effect on a large space.

The dislike of smoking has increased over the last decade as more people have given up the habit, and public opinion, not to mention legislation, now seems to be firmly against smoking in public places. Many organisers now insist that the conference room is designated a no smoking area, for the comfort and health of the majority, but compensate by scheduling regular breaks so that smokers do not feel victimised. Another solution is to designate areas of the room as smoking areas, and this can be successful as long as the flow of any air-conditioning or ventilation does not waft the smoke over the non-smokers.

Noise intrusions should also be a consideration. Late arrivals can be a problem but the disturbance can be minimised in some instances by putting 'Reserved' notices on the back two or three rows and then removing these as soon as the event starts.

Any telephones in the room should be disconnected and removed, and the question of the venue's paging and piped-music system should be raised. At one London hotel seminar, delegates were treated to regular calls for hotel staff put out by the front desk, and a meeting at another in a bar area, not usually rented out for events, was interrupted by intrusive music which could, it transpired, only be switched off for the whole hotel. Some temporary noise intrusions can be opportunities for speaker humour. At one event held in York, a delegate's portable telephone started to ring loudly. The speaker hardly broke his stride to say, 'If it's for me tell them I'll call back!'

Other considerations

Delegates should feel that they are the most important element of the conference, because they *are* the most important element. All efforts should be made therefore to ensure that their participation is a pleasurable and rewarding experience.

Delegates should be welcomed as they arrive at the venue – the 'meet and greet' – and quickly made to feel part of the event. This can be done by skilled reception staff who smile sincerely, use the delegates' names and fuss over them a little, taking coats and bags, pinning on badges and pouring coffee. Research carried out in the USA indicates that eye contact, and the simple act of touching a delegate to attach a badge, shake hands or simply touch an arm can considerably increase the feeling of belonging, of being 'included'. The wise organiser recognises that delegates attending events are away from the familiarity of their normal routine and their office. They are working a longer day and eating and drinking more than normal in (probably) grander surroundings than normal. Some find this stimulating, others may be overawed by it all and need a little cossetting.

With this in mind, any delegate packs given out should contain all the infomation needed to make attendees quickly feel at home. These should include a full programme, short biographies of the speakers, a list of other delegates, if relevant, as well as writing paper, and a pen or pencil. Supporting material might consist of transcripts of speeches, tickets for social events, vouchers for 'dine-around' programmes, and a welcome letter from the organiser or programme chairman.

Delegates on residential courses where they are paying their own bills, or even just for 'extras', will need to be advised of the charges made by the venue. One especially troublesome item is the cost of telephone calls, nearly always a very lucrative profit centre for hotels, as they are advised by telephone sales staff that by charging a healthy mark-up, sometimes five or six times the commercial rate, they can recover their capital cost in less than a year. Delegates should be advised to use their own portable phones, the public phones in the hotel lobby or to call a number and request someone to call back. One simple method is to call and let it ring for a pre-arranged number of times which means, 'I've arrived' or 'call me now'.

Another excessive mark-up is made on the mini-bar installed in many hotel rooms. Drinks from this commonly cost three or four times the price charged at off-licences, and delegates wanting to drink would be well advised to bring in their own. Hotel bars are not generally known for low prices either and delegates who like to drink a lot will be quickly sobered up by the bill in the morning.

Another potentially troublesome area involves telephone messages left at venue receptions for delegates and not passed on. A system must be put in place to ensure that such messages are treated with the importance they deserve. Ideally, callers should be put through to a member of the organiser's staff who can take a message and pass it on to the delegate in question at the earliest opportunity. If this is not possible, it is important to impress upon the hotel staff that a lost message, or an unnecessarily long delay in passing it on, reflects badly on both the event and the venue. One organiser at a Birmingham hotel, having done this, arranged for one of her friends to phone at 9.30 a.m. on the day of the event and leave a message, as a test, to call back 'as soon as possible'. The message was passed on at 12.45 p.m. and the organiser never used the hotel again as a result.

On the subject of telephones, some organisers make an outside line available to delegates attending their conferences and this is often much appreciated. Others distribute small change or phone cards free to enable delegates to make quick use of the hotel public telephones. There may, of course, be the occasional delegate who abuses the kindness by making long-distance calls on the organiser's telephone. Fortunately such instances are rare and most delegates behave in a more considerate manner.

Finally, it is important to treat delegates as the busy people they are. Some will have travelled considerable distances, or given up a night at home to be at the event in time for the opening, so *always* start on time. The only acceptable reasons for not doing so would be difficulties caused by bad weather, a strike by public transport workers or the disruption of transport due to terrorist activity. On these occasions the agreement of the audience should be sought before any timings are changed.

Post-event activity

It is essential to find out what the delegates thought of the event: the presentation itself, the presenters, the accommodation, the food and the venue. A well-thought-out evaluation form, usually best filled in by delegates before they leave, is one of the most effective ways of doing this. The forms can of course be confidential by not requiring a delegate's name and can simply ask that boxes are ticked to indicate opinions. This may be desirable if delegates are being asked to evaluate company speakers who are in a position of authority over them. Very few, it seems, will write that their chairman needs a course in presentation skills before appearing in front of a live audience again, or that their sales director's enthusiastic presentation was utterly unconvincing, but an anonymous form, with properly structured questions, can reveal this, to everyone's ultimate benefit.

Some companies, concerned that their events are less effective than they should be, are having outside consultants conduct confidential conference 'audits'. One Japanese company, carrying out such an audit, discovered that after a costly three-day event for its dealers, less than two per cent had grasped the main message of the conference and that most of the delegates rated the networking with other dealers the most useful of all the aspects. Some constructive changes were made to future events.

If the evaluation forms do not have to be confidential, it is easier to ask for specific suggestions for improvements and additions. Useful questions to ask might include:

1 On a scale of 1–10, how did the event fulfil your expectations?

2 Will you use any of the information? If so, what?

3 What, for you, were the most useful or enjoyable parts?

4 The least useful?

5 What could have been added to have made the event more useful or enjoyable?

6 On a scale of 1–10, how would you rate the food served?

7 Any complaints?

8 On a scale of 1–10, how would you rate the venue?

9 The accommodation?

10 Will you recommend this event to others?

The answers to the above can shape the way subsequent events are put together. At worst, the filling in of such a form can act as a safety valve for delegates with a grievance. Most organisers will take little notice of a specific complaint from one delegate – some of whom are habitual complainers who cannot be pleased – but a lot of notice if two or more complain or comment about the same thing.

Points for Discussion

1 Devise a programme for a two-day educational event, using as many presentation methods as possible. List start and finish times for each section.
2 Make a check-list of items to be sent to delegates before they attend.
3 You are organising a seminar on the subject of running conferences. Devise a form that delegates complete and send in before attending, one that would give useful information about the attendees, and provide useful points for discussion.
4 How should delegates be prepared for the possibility of a life-threatening emergency?
5 Devise a delegate's evaluation form for the event described in question 1.

CHAPTER SIX

THE

SPEAKERS

For many in the UK conference industry, the 1980s saw less emphasis on the real content at events, more on the medium used. The term 'talking heads' was disparagingly applied to any succession of speakers, mostly by audiovisual companies anxious to sell their latest state of the art equipment. 'Chalk and talk' was replaced by lasers, video, multi-screen projection, dry ice and fireworks. Speakers were replaced by presenters as substance gave way to style. The medium became the message as delegates were force-fed an American-style 'experience'. Information and ideas were pushed in, rather than drawn out and entertainment first supported the motivational aspects, then replaced them.

The slump of the 90s, and the resultant budget cuts, have sharply focused the minds of conference organisers back on to the objective for having the gathering in the first place. Smaller audiences and more interactive and participative sessions are back in vogue.

Although there will always be a place for the creative use of audiovisual effects, especially in the area of sales rallies and product launches with large audiences, the pendulum does seem to be currently swinging in favour of discussion, debate and delegate involvement.

Such sessions call for a different type of speaker, one perhaps more used to running training sessions than speaking at motivational events. 'Facillitators' may be more appropriate than 'presenters'. The sourcing and selection of appropriate speakers has always been an important part of an organiser's job, and is perhaps more so at the current time. Negotiation with speakers and the organisation and administration associated with using them is also important. Some thought may need to be given to training speakers since, even if the event uses no outside contributors the company presentation will be much enhanced by a better standard of delivery by all company executives, and it is often the more senior who all too clearly need the coaching.

Making a choice

The choice of speaker can make or break an event. 'Showbiz' types can look and sound great on television where they have a script, props and a supportive crew, but most do not have a cabaret act. Many do not transplant well into the real world where they have to put across their own views from a simple lectern, in front of a live questionning audience, and with no chance of another 'take' if it all goes wrong. As a number of organisers have found out, many personalities are prone to sell or plug their books or shows: the conference is regarded as just another sales opportunity, like most TV chat shows.

Organisers should also realise that the showbiz persona is invariably just an act, especially where comedians are concerned, and some very funny people on TV can be terribly serious, even boring, face to face.

Having said this, there are those stars of stage and screen who have specialised in the world of conferences, such as Bob Monkhouse, Nick Ross, Sue Lawley, Lance Percival and Janet Brown. Most will tailor their presentation to the audience and involve some of them, often with amusing results. Margaret Thatcher impressionist Janet Brown, hired to open the Telford Exhibition Centre in 1992, made the Labour MP for Telford, who was present in the audience, stand up, telling him, 'I won't shake hands, if you don't mind. I don't want the rest of your life to be an anti-climax.' Others have, by arrangement of course, lampooned chairmen, managing directors or key executives in companies, or officers of the association, for entertainment.

Such personalities usually have agents or work through speaker bureaux for their bookings (a list of sources can be found in Appendix 4 on page 152). Many organisers like to work through bureaux, especially if a lot of speakers need to be found. Also, if a chosen speaker is suddenly

Janet Brown impersonating Margaret Thatcher at the Telford Exhibition Centre
(*Source*: Telford Exhibition Centre)

unavailable then it is the job of the bureau, not the conference organiser, to find a replacement. On the other hand, organisers have found that if the opportunity exists to approach the speaker and book them directly, considerable savings can be made. Organisers should also note that when booking 'stars', the additional costs can be considerable since they may have special riders or clauses in their contracts which entitle them to bring a retinue of helpers and have special sound and lighting arrangements (often a moving spotlight) and dressing room facilities. Invariably, the contract states that their cabaret act may not be recorded.

Because of the relatively high cost, stars are often used as keynote speakers where a short presentation (30–60 minutes) sets the tone or theme of the whole conference. In the USA, sports personalities are also popular for this function, where they usually deliver a speech of the 'against-the-odds-we-still-won-through' inspirational variety, ideal for sales conventions.

Perhaps less inspirational are politicians who commonly have a standard speech, usually read (to avoid being misquoted), that they use for each occasion. One industry observer has suggested that all speeches by politicians to business groups follow the same framework:

1 'It's an honour to be here.'

2 'These are difficult times for you.'

3 'You have all coped magnificently'.

4 'There is no government money for you.'

5 'Have faith in the future.'

6 'Thank you for an excellent meal.'

This is, of course, a rather cynical view. Some politicians can be an asset to a conference, their name on the programme being a substantial attraction to potential attendees. Organisers should choose, however, with care and bear in mind that the politics of the politician may not find sympathy with a proportion of the audience. It should also be borne in mind that politicians are notoriously unreliable, in terms of actually showing up for engagements.

The Royal Family are another option for certain events, generally where the subject is one in which they have a genuine interest, or there is a strong charitable aspect. Princess Anne spoke at the opening of the 1992 Public Works Conference and then toured the attached exhibition talking to delighted exhibitors, an extra and much appreciated bonus for the organiser.

Experts in a given field will be the choice of many organisers for the bulk of a conference. Some fields have a clutch of 'known' speakers from which to choose and they will often be the safest bet. The disadvantage may be that their views are already well known and some delegates may have been exposed previously to the material, either at another conference or in published articles. In this respect the 'lesser expert' might bring in fresh and hitherto unexposed ideas.

There are a number of ways to find both experts and lesser experts. Authors of books on the subject, especially new books, are a logical starting point. They will also know many other experts in the field and will be a useful source of information, as well as being potential

HRH Princess Anne speaking at the 1992 Public Works Conference (*Source*: Apollo Photographers Ltd)

speakers. A word of warning though; when using authors remember that the written word and spoken word are two very different forms of communication: authors don't always make great speakers. They may also plug their books.

Editors of trade magazines and specialist columnists for national and local newspapers should also be able to help, as should officers in relevant trade associations and heads of relevant departments at colleges and universities. Speakers, once found, will invariably know others in the same field and this source should be thoroughly exploited.

One way of finding experts is through the 'call for papers' common with academic, scientific and medical events. The conference theme is announced and publicised and speakers are invited to submit their ideas and outlines. The practice has fallen out of favour with some of the better speakers because organisers have simply used it as a source of free ideas and the level of speaker attracted by such an invitation has been found to be less than satisfactory.

There are, of course, those who make a living by simply speaking, and their polished performances can enhance an event, especially for the keynote or after-dinner occasion. Many will properly tailor their material to the occasion although some, and often they are amongst the ones who demand the highest fee, simply deliver their 'canned' speech which may not be wholly suitable or relevant.

Finally, there are the inspired choices which can, on certain occasions, deliver a happy result. One conference organiser, David Seekings, notes that a speaker from the factory shop floor enthralled a group of senior executives, and others have at least held the attention of such audiences with controversial trade unionists. As a more bizarre example, a few years ago, it was popular for organisers of events in Rio to hire the fugitive thief, Ronald Biggs, to speak for the entertainment of delegates. Clearly the choice is as wide as the organiser's imagination.

Evaluating speakers

There really is no substitute for hearing a speaker speak as reputations and recommendations can sometimes be misleading. It should also be remembered that reading a prepared 20 minute speech to 1000 people is significantly different to addressing 20 people in a three-hour workshop format, with questions and interaction.

Some questions that the organiser might ask are:

1 Can the speaker achieve rapport with an audience? (Some top experts are arrogant, patronising and talk down to audiences.)

2 Does the speaker have experience of the particular audience and the presentation format?

3 Will the speaker answer questions? Or allow disagreement and debate?

4 How does the speaker present the material? Simply read a speech? Work from cue cards? Without any notes at all? Using slides, an OHP or video etc?

5 Are there references available? Audio- or videotapes of previous performances?

Negotiating with speakers

Some outside speakers will want £20 000 for a 30 minute appearance: others will waive any fee and even pay their own expenses to have a platform. For the organiser with a budget to meet it is worth bearing in mind some of the aspects which may help to reduce the fee charged.

1 Does the speaker have books, video tapes, audio tapes and other materials to sell at the event? These can provide a good source of income to the speaker, and some useful extra materials for the delegates.

2 Is the audience of commercial interest to the speaker? Most speakers receive bookings for new engagements as a result of being seen. Organisers can stress this, and even offer to supply a list of delegates.

3 Is the audience of commercial value to the speaker's company or organisation? One speaker, a director of a direct mail company admits, 'I'm being paid to sell.'

4 Is the rest of the conference of interest to the speaker? Many speakers will welcome the chance of attending the whole conference, to incease their own knowledge of the subject by listening to other speakers, talking to other delegates etc.

5 Is the publicity for the conference going to help the speaker? Often substantial publicity, in the form of direct-mail is valuable to speakers who can include copies of it in their portfolios as a third-party recommendation. Also helpful are any radio, TV or press interviews set up for speakers, and publicity in the various media afterwards.

6 Will the session be audio- or videotaped? Speakers often use copies of such recordings for their own publicity purposes.

7 Can the speaker carry out any other business in the area?

8 Would the speaker like to spend some extra leisure days at the conference destination? Or bring a partner? Often the cost of such extras is small to the organiser, but of considerable value to the speaker.

9 Has the speaker ever visited the conference destination? Some speakers, especially if invited to travel overseas, are happy to drop the price for a first visit, and fit in some leisure time.

10 What are the leisure possibilities at the destination? Some speakers will be influenced if there is the chance of persuing their favourite leisure activity, whether it be golf, scuba-diving, sailing or gambling.

11 Can the speaker conduct more than one session? Speakers will often charge very small extra amounts to perform more than once, on the basis that the main costs have already been covered.

12 Are there other ways the speaker would like to be paid? Some speakers are happy to take home a case or two of wine, which can often be written off by the organiser as part of the food and beverage cost of the conference. (Speakers should always be advised that such benefits of this kind must be declared to the relevant tax authorities.)

13 Is this event the only one organised or could there be others? Speakers often discount fees for a series of engagements.

Other points to bear in mind are that some speakers will be happy to speak for no fee because they genuinely want to help, and others will want fees donated to charity. Some may not be allowed to charge, and others, particularly in the scientific and academic worlds are happy just to have their papers published.

It is also worth remembering that speakers hired for a conference do talk to each other and will often compare notes on fees. There must always be a good reason for paying one less than another. Some organisers have found themselves losing speakers when an illogical inconsistency of payments has been discovered.

Approaching speakers

The most common first approach is a letter outlining the basics of the event (conference theme, date, time) with an invitation to make telephone contact, or a promise that subsequent contact will be made. Such a letter can flatter the speaker, stressing the importance of their contribution to the audience, the industry and the future of the world! It can also mention other speakers who have already agreed to participate, often helpful in persuading the speaker to speak.

The next logical stage will be a telephone conversation, prior to a meeting. Speakers will need then to gain further information about the event, as detailed below:

Audience type/level
Will the speaker feel comfortable with the level of audience? Will the material go above their heads or be beneath them? Will the speaker be speaking to peers? Competitors? A supportive or possibly hostile group? Potential employers or customers?

Audience size
Will the presentation be fully staged, with slides or videos and a large audience of up to 500? Or will it be a fully interactive small group of 20, needing written exercises? Alternatively, will it be a group of 50 people who could be happy with a flip chart and an OHP?

Promotion
As already noted, the promotion given to an event both prior to it and afterwards can be a significant benefit to a speaker. Most will want details of such activity. Some may want to amend their material if the press will be present, and some may even refuse to speak if this is so.

Length of presentation
Some will charge the same for a three-hour session as for a half-hour one. Others may want to be able to move on to another event where they can charge another fee and may therefore price the short talk more competitively. Time considerations will, of course, take into account any rehearsal time needed.

Fees and expenses
As previously noted, these aspects are highly negotiable. Most speakers however have a minimum total package in mind and will need to know whether or not the organiser's budget will cover this. Some may charge

more to speak to the larger audience, having already shrewdly assessed the size of their market.

Once agreement has been reached there will be a number of items that the organiser may need to consider:

1 *Speaker's 'bio'* Most conferences will include a short biography of the speaker in the delegate packs. This is invariably supplied by the speaker.

2 *Speaker's AV requirements* Some discussion needs to take place with regard to audiovisual needs: does the speaker need flip charts, OHPs, carousels, video players and monitors or an automatic cue system? Will there be any handouts to photocopy? If the speech is after lunch or dinner will a table lectern be needed for notes?

3 *Script* Will the speaker use a script? Can a copy of this be obtained in advance? If not can a summary be supplied, for use in the programme?.

4 *Permission to record/videotape* Speakers may not allow their performances to be recorded and this aspect should be discussed.

5 *Deadlines* The organiser will have deadline dates by which the materials and information as above need to be received.

There may also be other topics for discussion and negotiation such as travel arrangements, special dietary requirements, partners accompanying speakers, method and timing of payment and so on.

Once all this has been agreed, it is normal for the organiser to send a confirmation letter, detailing all the points and then wait for the speaker to respond. Once the booking has been confirmed, arrangements can then be made for the care of the speaker both prior to, and whilst at, the event.

The scope of these arrangements can be as broad and elaborate as the organiser wishes and will depend on the status of the speaker as well as on the budget available. Travel arrangements may be made by the organiser, and details of the venue and destination forwarded, along with press cuttings relating to the promotion of the event. If speakers are bringing partners, arrangements can be made for their inclusion in any special programmes being organised, should they wish. Speakers can be pre-registered for the event, to save them registering on arrival. They can also be met at the airport (in the US this is a sign of respect) chauffeur driven to the hotel, booked into a luxury suite equipped with welcoming fruit and flowers, complimentary champagne, conference details and local newspapers, and then whisked off to a cocktail party where they can meet the conference chairman and other VIPs.

Speakers will always appreciate a briefing room or 'ready room' where they can check their slides and OHP transparencies (and store them safely) sit and chat to other speakers and enjoy some light refreshments whilst waiting their turn. Some organisers are able to arrange for the conference sessions to be transmitted into the speaker's room. Speakers also appreciate the opportunity, if it can be arranged, to spend some time in the room in which they are going to speak, to familiarise themselves with the environment, the lectern and the audiovisual equipment. Those rehearsing will, of course, automatically gain this advantage.

The actual briefing of speakers on the day will vary from event to event. There are a number of accepted signals used by organisers which can mean 'speed up', 'slow down' or 'two minutes left' and these will need to be explained (see Chapter Eight). Information such as where the speaker will sit until called, which lectern they will use and where they will enter and leave the stage will also need to be given at the briefing.

Contingency plans

The organisation of any event carries with it the chance of an unforeseen hiccup. One medical conference in Aberdeen Scotland was disrupted when most of the surgeons left, quite rightly, to attend to those injured in the Piper Alpha oil rig disaster which happened during the conference. On another occasion, the guest speaker was due to be Terry Waite, the Archbishop of Canterbury's special envoy, who was kidnapped the night before the event.

However, the prudent organiser will have insured against such possibilities.

For operational problems there are a number of possible solutions, and some preventative measures, which can be considered by the organiser.

1 It is worth telephoning every speaker a few days before the event to make sure they are still coming.

2 If speakers are flying, they should carry their slides, OHP transparencies and precious notes as hand baggage and not check them in as luggage for the hold. Any material that can be copied and sent in advance to the organiser should be.

3 It may be a false economy to refuse to pay for a hotel room which would allow the speaker to arrive the day before. Any travel problems will thus be ironed out during the speaker's time, not whilst your delegates are sitting waiting for the speaker to arrive.

4 A meeting with the speakers the night before can be a good idea, in terms of creating some cameraderie and ensuring that all speakers are in place for the event itself. Don't expect too much discussion of the conference material however; most speakers have learnt from bitter experience not to reveal their ideas to others after having to listen with dawning horror as one of their 'friends' of the night before uses some of their best ideas when speaking, or when being interviewed by the press.

5 If a speaker is late, it may be that the programme can be rearranged to present them at a different time. If one does not turn up at all there are a number of possible solutions.

a Have someone else present their material (an understudy).

b Hold a panel session on the issues that were to be raised, with audience interaction.

c Have another speaker tackle a different, but relevant subject.

d Have a video to show, in case of such an emergency.

e Close up the programme to allow for the lack of speaker. Most delegates won't mind a longer coffee break or one of the other speakers taking more questions.

A good chairman, in such situations, will smooth things over and minimise the adverse impact on the audience. At one event attended by the author, the principal speaker, a radio scriptwriter had been talking for 10 minutes when he suddenly stopped, turned pale, said, 'Excuse me please' and bolted from the room. The chairman smoothly explained hat the speaker would soon be back and conducted an impromptu but excellent interactive question and answer session on the issues previously raised. After 10 minutes, the speaker returned explaining that he had eaten a partially reheated casserole the night before and had developed, as he put it, 'an unusually keen interest in lavatorial architechture', which got him a laugh, a good deal of audience sympathy and a standing ovation at the end of his session.

It might also be worth considering having spares of essential equipment standing by. At one marketing event, the carousel slide projector broke down. The speaker, a man of considerable experience and knowledge, explained to the horrified organiser that they had to get another one since he used his slides as cues and couldn't possibly function without them.

Nearly an hour later, a replacement was brought in and only then was the speaker able to continue.

Training speakers

It must not be assumed that all speakers are good at speaking. It's a big area where there is always something to learn and some of the best performers send themselves on regular training sessions to improve.

For the conference organiser there may be a problem: how to tell speakers who clearly need training tactfully that they do. Some may be senior personnel from within the organisation and some may be top experts in their field. Such stars may not take kindly to such suggestions.

One way around the problem has been found by some organisers who publish a set of speaker notes. These contain a wealth of hints and tips as well as a suggested reading list.

Another solution is to hold a speaker briefing session and have a speaker trainer come in to run it. Alternatively, details of forthcoming speaker training courses can be sent, perhaps with details of special discounts negotiated by the organiser.

Whatever method is used, it is essential that all performers at the event deliver their talks to a high standard. For the conference organiser to supply anything less is an insult to the audience and will seriously undermine the quality of the conference in their eyes.

Points for Discussion

1 What are the pros and cons of using celebrities? Politicians? Authors? A bureau?
2 How could you evaluate a speaker before a meeting?
3 If you were a speaker how would you sell yourself to an organiser?
4 What non-cash incentives could you explore to get speakers as cheaply as possible?
5 What makes a good speaker?

CHAPTER SEVEN

FOOD AND BEVERAGES

The food and beverages (F & B) offered to conference delegates can be, for the conference organiser, as important as the information, education, inspiration and motivation served up in the sessions.

Reasons for this are not hard to find.

In the first instance the act of eating together indicates a relationship between people, a sociability, which is most desirable to foster. The consuming of good food and drink is a pleasurable experience, a treat for most (whilst many may not actually live to eat, very few simply eat to live) and in providing this pleasure the conference organiser is contributing significantly to the delegates' sense of well-being, the 'feel good' factor. Food breaks provide a refreshing contrast between the more cerebral activities of listening, talking or discussing and the physical ones of getting up, moving around, and eating, all of which further stimulate the brain. The occasions are opportunities for conference organisers to be creative, original and to make the whole event more memorable. Last, but certainly not least, they are opportunities actually to improve the delegates' performance through a careful choice of menu.

Perhaps it is trite but true to say that a good event will feed the mind, body and spirit. Certainly, like in many things, the agreeable results obtained when this is achieved proves once again that the whole is greater than the sum of the parts. Alas, also very true is the fact that a failing in one area will affect the others; try serving a bad meal during the most informative and inspirational of conferences and watch morale, and retention, plummet.

Getting the food side right however is not simply a matter of picking the best hotel in town and the most expensive menu.

The food served must first be right for the delegates. Conference organisers are not always the best judges of such matters. Some, particularly those very new to the job or very junior will carefully choose the meal they know their boss will like. Others, like blasé film critics, see and experience so much that they slavishly search for something different, while their public are queuing up for more of the same. One UK venue agent has even suggested that such popular dishes such as pâté maison, prawn cocktail, *coq au vin*, steak, and black forest gateau should be purged from all conference menus for being too boring. In fact, in survey after survey of UK consumers' eating habits, the favoured meal of those eating out has, for the last 10 years, been prawn cocktail, grilled steak *garni* and black forest gateau, the last with just a dash of cream.

Even if delegates are above average in their food habits many may still prefer 'good food, plainly cooked, and plenty of it' rather than the small portions and fancy sauces that typify the *nouvelle cuisine* so popular with hoteliers and restaurateurs, and provide a fine example of culinary form over content.

All this is not to say that conference organisers should become traditionalists and never change. Indeed there are some important trends in eating that must be taken into account. There is a definite emphasis on healthier eating and drinking; a switch to high-fibre dishes, more 'natural' foods, more raw vegetables, less red meat, more white meat and less alcohol. More fish is being eaten as the value of fish oil in the diet is recognised.

Generally speaking, people are becoming more adventurous in their eating habits, often because of having travelled and experienced more foods, or just because they are eating out more. Attending a formal banquet in Maastricht, Holland in 1992, a group of conference organisers were presented with a starter of thinly sliced and marinated raw steak. Initially apprehensive, all who tried it pronounced it delicious and claimed that they would definitely serve it in similar circumstances.

Such creativity may need to be tempered however. On another occasion in the late 80s a conference organiser chose a meal for 50 other conference organisers and served a whole poussin (a small chicken) on each diner's plate as a main course. There were several objections to eating a whole trussed bird like that and it must be remembered that many people have become sensitive to the idea of killing animals, birds or fish for food and don't wish to be so graphically reminded of this. The same poussins boned, chopped up and simmered in a white wine and cream sauce with herbs would not have given offence. In fact, such a dish would probably be a good, if rather obvious, choice for a conference and it is worth, at this point, noting the criteria that might be considered by the conference organiser when planning meals.

General

Over the last few years there has been a growing realisation that the performance of delegates and their ability to retain information could actually be affected by the food and drink that they were given. On the simplest level, this began with an acceptance that people have a daily biorhythm. Their performance peaks at around 11.00 a.m., drops off sharply from about 1.00 p.m. to around 3.00 p.m. and picks up again by 6.00 p.m.

Thus drinking alcohol and eating heavy, starchy foods at lunchtime is more likely to produce torpor than euphoria for the afternoon sessions as the alcohol goes to the brain and the stomach struggles. Better at lunchtime are light, easily digested high-protein dishes, which give a delayed-action release of energy, with no alcohol, followed perhaps by a coffee. Thus the light chicken or fish lunch with lots of fruit juice came into being. This, in the recession of the early 90s evolved into the soup and sandwich, or soup and salad lunch, especially if delegates had a large hotel breakfast and would be enjoying a hotel dinner. For dinners, of course, the above can be reversed. Aperitifs and several types of wine can flow, meats in rich sauces with two vegetables and three types of potato can be enjoyed along with some wonderful steamed puddings covered in custard, all followed by chocolates, petits fours, a fine port or brandy and a long sleep before the next day's rigours begin!

Another way of sensibly affecting delegates normal biorhythms are serving a high-fibre, high-protein breakfast with lots of toast, rolls, cereals, fruit, cheese, eggs and meats and saving the lunchtime dessert until the afternoon tea break to give an immediate burst of energy to finish the day, an approach that saves money too.

As one American conference organiser, Rudy Knight, sums it up, 'What you eat is how you think.'

Specific conference factors

There are a number of other factors that will affect the actual choice of dishes made for a conference lunch or dinner. The fact that 200 people have to be served at once will rule out a lot of dishes that can only really be produced in small numbers, such as sautéed, grilled or flambéed items. The fact that food may need to be kept hot if the conference over-runs will mean that meat and fish in sauces will be favourite choices as these dishes are safer to keep due to the high temperature at which they can be maintained without spoiling. Certain vegetables, such as mange-tout, carrots and French beans keep their colour and texture, especially if cooked *al dente* (crisp) to begin with. However, the limited time available for a lunch might be against a salmon steak or whole trout being served up which will keep delegates happy for hours, picking out the bones.

Costs too will have an impact. Seafood is invariably expensive, even at venues by the sea, and game, duck and beef may also be out of the price range. Chicken, pork, lamb and some fish usually price out best of all and for those that need a cheap white meat dish suitable for most delegates, the ubiquitous chicken usually emerges supreme.

Another aspect of catering for large numbers is the growing trend towards vegetarianism. Around 7 per cent of UK conference delegates ask for a vegetarian option, although this figure varies with the region, and the age, sex and socio-economic category of delegate. A small percentage of these will be vegans, who eat no animal or fish products at all, and sauces will have to be checked to make sure that they are not meat based.

Other dietary problems which may be encountered by the conference organiser are allergies to certain foods (commonly shellfish, milk, eggs, wheat, bananas, tomatoes, strawberries, chocolate) and the various salt-free, gluten-free, low-cholesterol, diabetic and arthritic diets followed for medical reasons. Religious beliefs will also need to be taken into account. Muslims and Jews don't eat pork, which could also rule out beef Wellington or tournedos Rossini, both accompanied by pork liver pâté, and Hindus don't eat beef. Meats for Jewish and Muslim delegates will need to be kosher or halal (killed in the prescribed way). Many Roman Catholics don't eat meat on Friday.

Given the above as background, it is worth considering some of the specific meals and breaks in detail.

Breakfast

As noted, a substantial high-protein breakfast will improve delegates' performance. It will also reduce the need for a large lunch, perhaps cutting costs, since most delegates will not want three large meals a day.

It is also worth considering serving a breakfast of some kind even if the conference is non-residential. For a one-day event a breakfast will ensure that delegates arrive on time, have time to wake up and be alert for the sessions and have a useful opportunity to mix and mingle (network) before the conference starts. Even for a shorter event, a breakfast might be a good choice; a half-day event could start with breakfast at 8.00 a.m., with the session from 9.00 a.m. to 12.30 p.m. Again, this approach could save money since a breakfast is invariably a cheaper meal than lunch or dinner. This programming will also ensure that the material is presented during the part of the day when delegates will be at their most attentive and productive.

These days, the self-service buffet is the way that many venues offer breakfast and it has the considerable advantage of speed and choice. Those simply wanting a healthy continental-style breakfast, and increasing numbers do, can usually feast on cereals, croissants, pastries, rolls, toast, fresh and tinned fruits with yoghurts and a selection of cheeses and meats. Those wanting a more traditional English-style breakfast can help themselves to their fry-up.

The trend away from the fresh-cooked breakfast does not suit everyone and for some delegates the more traditional service is preferable, time permitting. Breakfast can also be made 'special'. One truly memorable and leisurely one-hour breakfast at a country hotel deep in rural Wales

(The Lakes Country Hotel) consisted of Welsh lamb sausages with mint and other herbs and sweetcured bacon, both from a local butcher, perfectly complemented by soft-cooked, scrambled, free-range eggs, local wild mushrooms and a slice of the traditional Welsh laver bread, which is a delicious mixture of Swansea seaweed and oats. Another memorable start to the day was held at a Devon hotel (The Saunton Sands Hotel) which serves a genuine American steak and hash browns breakfast for those organisers looking to give delegates a special treat. A barbecue breakfast outside can also add a special occasion touch.

If a buffet breakfast is served, then the hot and cold selections should be on separate stations, to save holding up delegates who only want one or the other.

Those looking to save money and waste can arrange for the fresh fruit, pastries, etc. left over to be offered at the mid-morning break.

Brunch

This American-style combination of breakfast and lunch is gaining popularity as it can save money and add a touch of something different to an event. It is particularly suitable as a goodbye meal or when delegates have had a late social event the night before. At one weekend conference at a Bristol hotel (The Bristol Marriott), there was a disco till 2.30 a.m., a light hot supper till 3.30 a.m. and a New Orleans style 'Jazz-brunch' at 11.00 a.m. the next morning, after a much needed lie-in. As well as the usual breakfast offering, delegates enjoyed steaks, cajun-style chicken, and a delicious combination of scrambled eggs and smoked salmon, all to the foot-tapping music of Dixieland.

Tea and coffee breaks

Usually held mid-morning and mid-afternoon, these offer delegates a chance to stretch their legs, quench their thirst, go to the toilet, discuss the conference issues with other delegates and phone the office. Sufficient time for these activities, usually 15–30 minutes, should be allowed. In some venues, the longer break is definitely a good idea; one organiser of a seminar held at a popular central London venue (The New Connaught Rooms) discovered that, due to the building's use as a centre for the male-dominated freemasonry movement, there were far fewer ladies toilets than mens. In fact, from the room being used, women on the course had a complicated three-minute walk to another floor to endure, there and back. The 15 minutes allotted for tea and coffee breaks was therefore too short and parts of sessions were missed. Another thief of valuable time for the organiser is the poor organisation of the way the refreshments are served when large numbers have to be catered for. Experienced organisers will have milk, sugar, biscuits, juice etc. on a number of separate tables, well away from where the black coffee or tea is being poured. This simple ploy can speed up the flow of delegates collecting their drinks by three or four times. The good organiser will also have someone warning the catering staff, 'They are just finishing, start pouring!'

For some large events it might be possible and preferable to have the breaks in the conference room with cups already laid out and coffee etc. brought in when needed. Small meetings can use drinks in flasks, which can keep the tea or coffee hot for hours and which can be poured by delegates as needed. One hotel group (Jarvis) sensibly supplies coffee mugs, rather than cups and saucers, to minimise noise. Certainly the break provides a chance for some exercise and there is no need, generally, to supply chairs to sit on, as it is much better that delegates walk around, circulate and talk to each other.

In terms of what is served during the break, many organisers now offer coffee and tea, white and brown sugar, decaffeinated coffee, juices and mineral waters. Some offer a range of teas: English Breakfast, Earl Grey, Orange Pekoe, Lapsang Souchong etc. Snacks can be simple or exotic. Standard packaged biscuits are becoming less popular now as the much nicer home-baked sorts come into fashion. The local speciality can also be represented: shortbread in Scotland, bara brith cake in Wales and so on. Pastries are generally the rather standard Danish sort but can also be small doughnuts, or chocolate croissants. Many organisers, mindful of the difficulties of delicately eating a large Danish pastry, have the hotel cut these in half to allow disposal in two or three bites and improve take up. The exception to this will be where the organiser has negotiated to pay by the tray (nearly always cheaper) in which case large sticky items will be consumed less readily than small ones. Healthy eaters will appreciate fresh fruit and cereal bars.

Organisers should not be afraid to specify such details as those above; every aspect of the event is important and deserves thinking through for maximum impact. At one UK event held during July, the organiser served Italian ice-cream cornets at the afternoon break, something the delegates still talk about, though the educational aspects of the event are largely forgotten. Another organiser, who used a frog as a logo for the conference, had a cake made in the shape of a frog, covered in green marzipan, and wheeled it in for consumption as delegates were drinking their afternoon tea and wondering if the usual biscuits had been forgotten. This gesture cost £100 for 200 delegates and underlined the conference theme again. It was certainly more memorable than serving custard creams and bourbons. In fact any decent baker will be able to make small cakes or biscuits to fit the theme, at little cost.

In addition to the break itself, some thought will need to be given to the method of getting delegates back into the sessions afterwards. Some favour the simple announcement, perhaps broadcast into the room. 'Ladies and gentlemen your next session will start in three minutes. Please make your way back to the auditorium.' Others suggest switching the lights on and off, to signal the end of the break.

Lunches

Lunch, whatever it comprises, can be served to delegates sitting at tables or it can be a self-service buffet. This latter option is generally the most popular. Delegates can choose to eat a lot or a little, as they wish, and the act of getting up to go to the buffet gives some exercise. The buffet selection can include some vegetarian dishes which can also be enjoyed by everyone: vegetable soups, quiches, salads, cauliflower cheese, vegetarian pastas and risottos, ratatouille etc. It's also the quickest way to serve food when time is limited, but a word of warning is necessary here: the logistics need to be carefully considered for large groups.

A well-stocked buffet table with only one serving point and 50 or more delegates to be served could be a disaster, because of the precious time taken up. A check on the queuing time at a buffet for 80 in a Central London hotel a few years ago was quite revealing. The choice was enormous and the last person in the queue waited a total of 38 minutes to get to the food. Consider that each delegate will spend around 30 seconds making a choice in such circumstances and the problem with 80 delegates becomes clear.

The first solution is to cut down the choice available. Second, the

A buffet layout (*Source*: New Quebec Quisine Ltd, London, W1)

organiser should insist on the buffet being split so that it is repeated, one such serving point per 40 delegates being about right. Having more waiters to serve would also help, as would putting the starters, main courses and desserts on obviously separate tables, with separate plates.

Another option is to specify the starter, a simple Florida cocktail or antipasto perhaps, and have this plated and ready on the table as delegates arrive. Hot or cold main course choices can then be available as a self-service buffet, as can the dessert. Since people eat at different rates the trips will be naturally staggered.

A mini-buffet can also be laid out on each eating table. In the USA a growing trend is the 'table-deli' whereby delegates sit at their tables and make their own sandwiches from a central selection, which is of course attractively laid out, a most important consideration; we eat through our eyes, noses and mouths, in that order.

Sometimes there are opportunities to do something a little different and make the lunch more memorable, by having it by a pool perhaps, or serving a barbeque outside. If the latter is chosen in the UK (and food *does* taste better in the open air) a contingency plan for a switch to inside eating needs to be in place, in case of rain. Even in hot countries, alfresco eating has its draw-backs. In Australia, a barbecue in the beautiful Blue Mountains was plagued by clouds of voracious mosquitoes, which significantly reduced the enjoyment. Back in the UK, a few dozen buzzing wasps at a barbeque drove delegates back inside to eat their food.

Remember also that food eaten standing up should be able to be eaten with the hands, like a hamburger or hot dog, or small enough to put on a fork or spoon and consume without cutting up. Large steaks therefore may not be suitable. Kebabs, where small pieces of beef, pork, lamb or chicken can be threaded and cooked on a skewer and then removed for consumption are a good solution. Prawns and mussels wrapped in bacon can also be cooked this way, and a vegetarian kebab can be made with mushrooms, tomatoes, peppers and onions.

The more informal 'stand up and circulate' lunch is the best option for most occasions where delegates want to talk to each other. Worst arrangement of all is that where, in a large and possibly noisy gathering, delegates are sat on round tables of 10, very common in hotels. It is generally impossible for them to talk to anyone except the people on their immediate left and right, with whom they are now trapped for an hour or more and may have nothing in common.

The normal time allotted for a full lunch would be one hour. Some time can be saved, and delegates got back to work, by serving the coffee back in, or just outside, the conference room.

Dinners, gala dinners and banquets

Dinners for conferences may be simple, informal and cheap, or elaborate, formal and very costly, to suit the occasion. Generally speaking the term 'gala dinner' denotes the last dinner of the event and a banquet is an elaborate formal dinner (or lunch). Both will undoubtedly feature more than three courses, a range of aperitifs, wines and liqueurs, and possibly include speakers, entertainment and awards ceremonies. Such events are often the climax towards which the whole conference programme is built.

The objective will usually be to make the meal a special occasion, certainly the best meal of the day and this will be accomplished by not only making sure that the food is right but by paying attention to all the

The Osbourne Room at the Brighton Metropole laid for dinner (*Source*: Brighton Metropole)

other aspects which influence a delegate's perception and the overall feel or atmosphere of the event. These will include the layout of the tables, the table linen, the flowers, the glassware, the cutlery, the china and the printed menus. Also given attention will be the lighting, the decoration of the room, the centrepiece and any background music. All these aspects, and the dress of the delegates, will create the right mood for the meal. At one London hotel (The Inn on the Park, now the Four Seasons) the banqueting manager put black cloths on all the tables, turned out the main lights and simply picked out the floral centrepiece on each table with a spotlight. Whilst some may feel that such a dramatic treatment would only be suitable for a gathering of undertakers, the point is that much of the mood of the delegates and their perception of the event will be influenced by the visual presentation and efforts should be made to ensure that all non-food aspects are taken into account. Some even feel that, given the constraints of bulk catering, these considerations are the more important.

Turning to the food itself, a formal or gala occasion gives conference organisers a real challenge, usually to provide something special but within budget. There are some points worth noting.

First, the dishes selected should offer a range of colours, shapes and textures. A main course comprising chicken in a white sauce with boiled potatoes, cauliflower and braised celery is depressingly boring in colour and texture. Bright yellow sweetcorn mixed with red and green peppers, bright orange baby carrots, crisp green mange-tout or French beans and crisp golden-brown roast or Parmentier potatoes would be better accompaniments.

Second, the dishes need to lend themselves to catering in bulk, bearing in mind the constraints of the venue's kitchen. Dishes that have to be flambéed at the table clearly have their drawbacks if 500 need to be served, as do sautéed or stir-fry ones. Complicated dishes, such as beef Wellington are a problem because they don't keep well, and in a hot kitchen baked Alaska, (ice-cream in a meringue) can melt very quickly.

Chefs will have their own personal nightmare as far as requests from organisers are concerned but, '500 mixed grills please' would figure high on the list of most, and some gourmets claim that fresh, sliced smoked salmon for the same number would be similarly impossible. As has already been noted, meat or fish in a sauce is a safe and sensible choice from the point of view of serving large numbers.

Third, the dishes should suit the talents of the staff. There is no point in talking chefs into preparing something they don't feel confident with. Better to ask them what they do best, and be guided by them.

In terms of specifics, consider local specialities, which may be inexpensive, memorable and liked by the delegates. In Scotland, a bowl of Cullen skink (fish soup) or an Arbroath smokie, (a smoked haddock) might make an appropriate starter. In Wales, the lamb is famous for its tenderness and flavour and in the West Country, a cream tea with scones, jam and cream could make an interesting dessert. During a trip to the Pennines, a group of conference organisers sampled some dock pudding, a local savoury dish made in the Calderdale area from dock leaves, breadcrumbs and herbs, another new food experience.

It is also perhaps worth knowing that quite a high proportion of a large group may not like some of the vegetables chosen. In a small survey carried out in 1991 amongst conference organisers by The Meetings Forum, 19 per cent said they didn't eat Brussels sprouts, 15 per cent didn't eat cabbage and 11 per cent didn't eat butter-beans. Parsnips, broad beans, peppers and aubergines were also mentioned as being disliked by some of the respondents.

The same group were also asked to choose a meat or a fish for a main course to be served at a gala dinner. Beef was chosen by 33 per cent, lamb by 26 per cent and duck by 26 per cent. Very few chose salmon or chicken and no one chose pork, veal or game. For some, the tastiest of meats, duck, is becoming ever more popular as ways of getting rid of the protective layer of fat that covers the breast are employed to produce a more acceptable meat dish. The duck served is generally the domesticated variety; wild duck has a strong flavour that is something of an acquired taste and a wild duck dish may contain shotgun pellets. Remember that gourmet tastes are not necessarily popular tastes. In some circles, a pheasant must be hung until 'gamey' and 'high' before eating. Stilton cheese is best when green rather than blue and Brie should be very runny. These strong tastes are unlikely to suit the majority.

Since 1991, there has been more interest in fish for special occasions, particularly the meatier varieties such as salmon, swordfish and tuna. Also being seen on special menus more often are monkfish (which tastes a little like lobster and is sometimes used as a scampi replacement) red snapper and kingfish (opah).

Also currently enjoying a revival are soups, which can be inexpensively made in a blender. Some unusual combinations can be presented such as tomato and gin, carrot and coriander and cream of leek and potato with stilton, this last served hot or cold. Crunchy croutons can be added for an extra touch.

Desserts for dinners can be a healthy fresh-fruit salad, or mousse. Increasingly acceptable, perhaps as a mild protest against the health food movement, are the more traditional sweet desserts: treacle pudding, fruit crumbles, spotted dick, bread and butter pudding etc. Chocolate is always a big favourite, usually as a sauce poured over profiteroles, (choux pastry balls filled with cream). Ice-cream with hot fruit pie is also much appreciated.

Dinners can be made more special, and longer affairs, by the simple addition of courses. A soup can be followed by a small fish course, then the main course. Or a sorbet, to clean the palate can follow the starter, especially if it is a strongly flavoured pâté, terrine or smoked fish. A cheese and biscuits course, perhaps with fresh fruit, can follow the dessert, and petits fours or chocolates can accompany the coffee. Remember that the extra courses will usually require extra cutlery and this may reduce the number of delegates that can be seated around one table.

Theming the event is something else to be considered; indeed many conferences will have an overall theme to be carried through all presentations and meals. One UK sales conference had an overall Wild West theme of 'Time for the Showdown' with one of its major competitors. Thus the sessions gloried in names like 'Saddle up' and 'Head 'em off', tea and coffee breaks were 'Trail stops' and the gala dinner, barbecue style was 'Steak your claim'.

The themes can be carried through with the colours and patterns of linen provided, the printed paper napkins and even ice sculptures, special table centrepieces and room decorations. Food can also be themed. Hotel consultant Derek Taylor recalls the 007 pasta numerals floating in soup for a James Bond party, and the macaroons with printed rice paper at the press event, where the journalists and editors were forced to 'eat their words'.

Receptions

Receptions are early evening functions which might precede a dinner, or replace it, in which case the food element will move from 'light nibbles' (nuts, crisps, canapés), to heavy hors-d'œuvres, or a full buffet.

When the reception precedes dinner it will usually be shorter, around an hour, enough time for two or three drinks and perhaps five or six hors-d'œuvres per person. It is important not to overdo the snacks on such occasions; many a good gala dinner has been ruined by prior overindulgence by delegates, in both food and drink.

In some instances, the delegates may or may not be going on to eat dinner individually and a reception with plenty of food can serve as dinner for some, and for those with iron wills, a small tasty appetiser before going out to dine. People vary in their capacity to eat of course, but generally 20–25 'pieces' of hors-d'œuvres per delegate would be a good estimate if the reception was to replace dinner.

For such receptions there are a number of points to bear in mind. The objective will be for people to mix and talk to each other and to this end there should be very few chairs available, in order to promote circulation. All foods should be easy to eat either with the fingers or with just a fork. To cut down consumption, make everything finger food and don't supply plates, knives or forks, just a napkin. Plates encourage people to load up and should, if supplied at all, be very small if the budget is a problem. To cut down on wastage, order hors-d'œuvres by the tray and don't have all the trays set out to begin with, but have fresh trays brought out as food is consumed, and spread the food available over the time allotted. Seafood is always the most expensive and the first to be eaten. To save costs, cut down on this or have it served with cheaper bulk food, seafood vol-au-vents for example.

Raw vegetable dips are ideal reception food, being cheap, colourful and healthy. Raw carrot, cauliflower, mushrooms and red and green peppers are all suitable along with celery, radishes, cucumber sliced longwise and baby tomatoes. Other favourites are small hot sausages to dip in a mustard or barbecue sauce, Indonesian satay (miniature meat and fish kebabs) to dip in a hot spicy peanut sauce and miniature spring rolls with a soy sauce. Other popular dips are guacamole, made with avocado, and salsa, made with onion and tomato.

Larger, more elaborate receptions can, like gala dinners, be themed. At one held by the Society of Incentive Travel Executives (SITE) in Dublin the theme was 'A taste of Ireland' and various stalls set up in the banqueting suite dispensed shell fish and smoked fish, soups and stews, carved joints, cakes, pastries, puddings and Guinness. At another November reception in Brighton, an organiser of a conference for the financial sector considered that his delegates had had lots of experience of *haute cuisine* and, for a welcome change, organised a party on the Palace Pier. The pier was closed to the public and delegates, entering a marquee set up on the end of it, were given an open bottle of champagne and a paper cup. Stalls outside served cockles, whelks and mussels as well as hamburgers, hot dogs, pizza and doughnuts. Despite the cold winter night delegates, fortified with champagne, entered into the back-to-childhood spirit, some even sliding happily down the helter-skelter.

At another successful reception, a Wild West themed event at the Holland Park Hilton, delegates enjoyed some down-home barbecue cooking washed down with a heady punch, and took the opportunity to ride a mechanical bucking bronco. Receptions can be much more informal affairs than gala dinners and for many, a lot more fun.

Dine-around programmes

Probably an American invention, these are ideal for giving delegates a chance to eat dinner away from the host hotel. Arrangements are made with local restaurants to honour vouchers printed, and these are then presented by the delegates in lieu of money. They can be for food only, or include drinks as specified.

The benefits to delegates, especially those attending a three-day or longer event, will be a break from hotel food, a chance to try a local restaurant and an opportunity to join up with a chosen group of other delegates for some all-important socialising.

Drink

As already noted, the serving of alcoholic drinks at conference lunches seems to be declining and the 'no alcohol before 6.00 p.m.' rule seems to be more widely followed as organisers enjoy the benefits of sober delegates in the afternoon sessions. There is also more awareness of the possibly fatal consequences of overindulgence for those delegates driving home afterwards, although sadly this message does not seem to have yet got through to some of our hoteliers and organisations that should know better. At the 1992 AGM of the UK Meetings Industry Association (MIA), the Forte-owned Grosvenor House Hotel in London annoyed some delegates by serving only doubles of spirits from the lunch-time bar.

As well as the undesirable personal dangers to delegates, there is also, particularly in the USA, the ever-present spectre of legal action for those who allow or encourage the overindulgence. At an association meeting in Oregon in 1984, one tipsy delegate staggered from the reception and ploughed his car into another. The victim in the other car suffered permanent hip damage and successfully sued the association in 1987 for $300 000. The association was forced into bankruptcy.

Even in the USA however, where there is a fairly high incidence of alcoholism, 35 per cent of the population is teetotal and another 30 per cent average only two drinks a week, according to the US-based Responsible Beverage Service Council. To cut down consumption they recommend:

- not allowing delegates to get bored – they drink more

- not serving salty snacks – as every barman knows these increase consumption

- serving high protein foods to slow alcohol absorption

- providing lots of soft drinks, non-alcoholic cocktails and low-alcohol beers

- not allowing the hotel to serve doubles

- shortening the time allotted for drinking, and replacing alcoholic drinks with coffees and teas before the end, to reduce the worst effects of the alcohol

- making sure that any delegates who are over the limit *don't* drive home – a taxi fare or a hotel room is a small price to pay as insurance against a possible fatal accident or a lawsuit

To the above it can be added that the room should be kept cool, and that a system where delegates pay for their own drinks might also reduce consumption. It might also be worth remembering that many organisers have noted the decrease in the alcohol consumption of men when their wives attend functions!

It is normal to run a drinks reception before dinner, to allow all delegates to muster and mingle before serving. This can also be a sherry reception, a cocktail reception (with perhaps a special 'themed' cocktail) or a champagne reception. The latter can be surprisingly inexpensive if the champagne is paid for by the bottle and a dry (sec) is specified since many people don't like it, and even those that do can rarely drink more than half a bottle.

If delegates are buying their own drinks then a cash bar is usually set up. Sometimes organisers will arrange a combination bar which is partly open in the sense that the first drink the delegates have is paid for by the organiser, the rest by the delegates. If this arrangement is made it must be clearly communicated. At one USA event, delegates cheerfully downed drink after drink, under the impression that the organiser was paying for all of it. There were some ugly scenes when bills were presented to delegates.

As a general guide allow three drinks per hour, more if the room is stuffy and/or salty snacks are provided. Drinks can be bought on a per drink, per bottle or per head basis and thought will need to be given as to the most appropriate arrangement.

A 70 centilitre bottle of spirit will yield 28 measures (25 millilitres each or approximately $\frac{1}{6}$ gill) in the UK. In the USA, a one litre bottle will yield 33 of the larger one ounce measures. A 75 centilitre bottle of wine will yield four to six glasses.

On the subject of wine, at dinner, especially at a gala dinner or banquet, it will be normal to serve a wine with the first course as well as one with the main course. It is generally accepted that the best wines should be served first – after a glass or two the palates of most people become less discerning. A general rule is to serve a white wine with fish and white meat (chicken, pork, veal, turkey) and a red wine with red meat (beef, lamb and game) but tastes and opinions vary. Certainly there is nothing wrong with serving a popular and perhaps well-advertised wine if it is appropriate and the majority of delegates are going to enjoy it.

If beef or pork is being served, which contains a fair amount of natural fat, then a drier wine may be more appropriate, to balance this. Generally, there is a preference of three to one in favour of white wines. If red is served remember that 'room temperature' is 50 degrees fahrenheit, (10 degrees celsius) the temperature of a cool cellar, not that of an overheated function room of a hotel. Light red wines such as Beaujolais and red Lambrusco benefit from a light chilling. French Cabernet Sauvignon is the most popular red, German Liebfraumilch the most popular white. One UK organiser delighted sophisticated delegates by serving an award-winning English wine. For those wishing to save money on wines most hotels have a 'house' wine that can be a good choice. Carafes of such wine can be a money saver. Just asking waiters not to refill glasses until asked can save considerable amounts, some say 40 per cent, if paying by the bottle. Local wines will nearly always be cheaper than imported ones, especially in wine-growing countries. If wine is paid for by the bottle then a conference sticker can be applied to bottles as they are opened. Being seen to check such details discourages abuse by hotel staff.

Those wishing to save money on drink generally might check the prices of liqueurs, especially vintage ports and brandies. One UK organiser allowed delegates a free choice and the drinks bill was far higher than that for the food, a common occurrence in luxury hotels. Mineral water can be very expensive as hotels exploit the popular fad for drinking it; jugs of iced tap water are usually as acceptable, and far cheaper in the UK, though perhaps a health hazard in some other European countries.

According to one gourmet, the best food choices for money saving are watercress soup, which apparently is so strongly flavoured that it kills the palate for any wine, a thick fatty steak, which only requires a cheap, rough red and a 'death-by-chocolate' style dessert, which like watercress, defies any wine choice at all!

Buying F and B

In terms of selecting an establishment that can serve a top-quality meal to a small group there are, fortunately, a number of guides on the market which have a good reputation for their independence and impartiality. As already stated, the *Egon Ronay* and *Michelin* guides are two that can be trusted as can the *Good Food Guide* published by the Consumers' Association.

An incognito visit is, as with the general selection of the venue, a good idea. Some experts claim that a lot can be learned by ordering a meat or fish dish cooked in a sauce and a pastry case, a choice which should demonstrate the varied skills of a good chef. Others advise to take note of the way vegetables are presented, and the quality of the cheese selection.

In the USA, and increasingly in the UK, it is common to insist on meeting the chef, inspecting the kitchens, (a good chef will be happy to show them off) agreeing on a suitable selection of dishes and then having a test meal, perhaps with a tasting of a selection of wines.

In terms of forecasting numbers this may be very easy for the organiser of the company event, but harder for the promoter of the commercial seminar, where 'no-shows' are more common. Banqueting managers at venues will want, understandably, to know final numbers at least two working days in advance.

From the organiser's point of view, an arrangement which gives a figure plus or minus 10 per cent is ideal, particularly for the organiser of the commercial event. Such an organiser expecting 250 may actually find that only 220 turn up for the day. The above arrangement would save over £1 000 in delegate fees in a central London hotel and is clearly worth considering. It is also worth noting that a buffet for 100 will invariably serve 120.

As well as a good selection of food and drink, the careful organiser will need to ensure that the hotel will supply enough waiting staff. At one meal in a London hotel in December 1992, over 200 guests were waited on by just four members of the banqueting team; unsurprisingly the main course took 45 minutes to serve.

As a guide, one waiter per 20 is about right for plated or silver service with one per 40 for a buffet.

In conclusion, there is probably no such thing as the 'perfect' meal, especially where a large number has to be fed. A near to ideal meal will be one that suits the delegates, the time of day, the occasion, the area, the time of year, the climate, the talents of the chef and the organiser's budget. It is something of a juggling act, but one well worth perfecting.

Food is important to conference delegates, and a bad meal is perhaps more memorable than a good one.

Points for Discussion

1 What are the main benefits of incorporating a meal into an event?
2 How have eating habits changed over the last 10 years?
3 How can food be varied to improve delegates' energy levels?
4 Plan three menus suitable for a luncheon and a gala dinner, using foods and dishes that you yourself would like to eat.
5 List a range of 20 dishes all suitable for a buffet for 100, taking into account vegetarian preferences.

CHAPTER EIGHT

AUDIOVISUAL EQUIPMENT

Audiovisual (AV) equipment is put to best use when it supports, reinforces, enhances, clarifies and improves retention of the message.

The choice of medium used will be governed by the audience, the occasion, the subject(s) and the budget. It will also be affected by the objective, whether this is to inform, educate, train, team-build, problem-solve, motivate, entertain, or a combination of these. As well as improving the presentation, audiovisual equipment, properly used, can ensure that all delegates properly hear and see the whole programme, a fundamental objective which is not always achieved.

Used badly, the audiovisual element can confuse and obscure the message. Talented and knowledgable speakers often spoil their presentations with poor slides or OHP acetates, and organisers are led down the expensive road of impact for impact's sake, or memorability at any cost. One managing director of an AV equipment rental company, selling his services to a group of conference organisers, bounded on to an empty stage dressed only in a pair of boxer shorts and a bow-tie, and proceeded to get dressed as his crew built a conference set around him. The performance was described by some as 'offensive' and by most others as 'just naff'. Perhaps more significantly, no one could remember what he actually said, although retention of the visual aspect was high. Having the chairman lowered down to the lectern on a rope amidst rolling smoke and the crashing chords of the 1812 Overture sounds like a great gimmick but will anyone then remember the main points of his presentation? To misquote Winston Churchill, never in the field of business communication is so little so often achieved, for so much.

Used well however, good visual impact can enhance what is being said, and markedly improve the memorability of the message, the whole point of the event in the first place. Some claim that we forget 80 per cent of what we hear but only 50 per cent of what we see and hear. Certainly, even still pictures such as bar charts or graphs can convey a lot of information. Moving pictures, as TV programme and film makers know, can convey even more. Imagine trying to describe how to perform the perfect golf swing, and how much easier it would be with a video clip, run in slow motion. The graphic treatment enhances universal understanding and improves retention.

The visual equipment used at an event will usually include, depending on the event's size, objectives, audience and budget, one or more of the following: flip charts, overhead projection, slide projection, video projection and screens.

Flip charts

Simplest of all the audiovisual options these are large paper pads mounted on easels. The pads can be drawn on by the presenter in a variety of coloured felt-tipped pens and the pages flipped over. As long as presenters write legibly in large block letters, flip charts are ideal for small audiences (up to 50 or 60) where interactive audience contribution or brain storming is the objective. Flip charts are cheap, portable and take up little space. Pages can be prepared prior to the event and can be removed and pinned on walls for further discussion. Also, notes can be made in faint pencil by the presenter (unseen by the audience) and used as prompts. One modern advance in flip-chart technology has produced a chart with white plastic acetate pages, which can be wiped clean and used again.

An alternative to the flip chart is the whiteboard. This has a permanent smooth white surface which is written on with special water-based coloured pens and the images removed with a cloth, a sensible successor to the old-fashioned blackboard and chalks. An even more modern version of the whiteboard is an electronic board which makes an A4-sized copy of whatever is written on it. However, in a lecture situation where delegates need a copy each, the process may be painfully slow and distracting.

A flip chart in use (*Source*: Acco Europe)

Overhead projectors (OHPs)

These are called 'Vu-graphs' in the USA and are projectors which, using an arrangement of light and mirrors, project an image printed on clear plastic acetate film on to a screen.

OHPs are very versatile and a firm favourite of many presenters. Individually prepared acetates ('foils') can be quickly and cheaply made

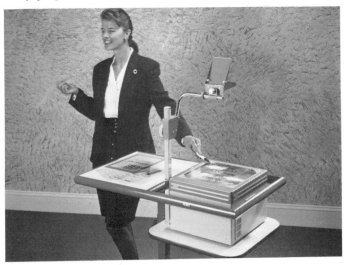

An OHP in use (*Source*: Nobo Visual Aids Ltd)

on a photocopier, or images can be drawn during the presentation, either on a succession of blank acetates or on a continuous roll fixed to the projector which can be wound on. The projectors are inexpensive, readily available, easy to operate and portable. Unlike slides, OHP images do not have to be viewed in blackout conditions.

As with a flip chart or white board, delegates can make contributions which can then be included immediately. Using overlay or masking techniques, a list of points can slowly be revealed, or a diagram built up. There are several disadvantages of using OHPs: some may be noisy (the lamps are cooled with fans), it is easy for acetates to get out of sequence, the unit may obscure the screen for some in a small group, the image quality is not brilliantly sharp, and it can be hard to get a squared image. This latter problem is referred to as 'keystoning' i.e. the base is narrower than the top, like the keystone of an old stone bridge.

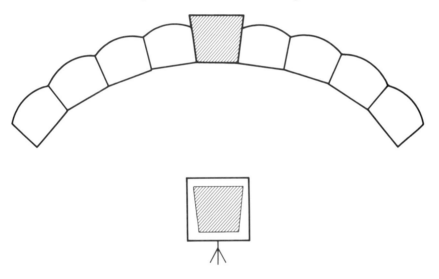

The effect of 'keystoning' on an OHP transparency

Also, as with anything electrical, fuses and bulbs can blow. Wise presenters ensure that they know how to change a bulb, and have a spare and a handkerchief ready (a blown bulb will be hot).

One modern use of the traditional OHP is to project data and graphics straight from a computer. This is done by using a liquid crystal unit mounted onto the projector.

Slide projection

Slides are a good medium to use for small or large audiences. They are quickly made, give a high-quality image and are very controllable as modern projectors incorporate a remote control facility. They can be originated on a personal computer (PC), and uses for them range from having a few in a projector operated by a speaker, to having thousands in banks of projectors driven by a computer and back-projected onto a screen, complete with a soundtrack. Thus, either very simple or highly complex and sophisticated presentations can be based around slides.

The main problems are that, unlike flip chart pages and OHP acetates, slides cannot be created on the day. Slides are thus a medium of presentation rather than interaction or involvement. In addition, the room needs to be blacked out to view slides properly, when using front projection.

In this case, delegates will be unable to make notes, eye contact with the speaker is lost, and darkness can induce sleepiness. Back-projected images do not need a blackout to view them.

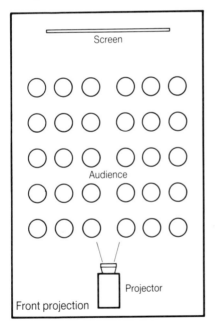
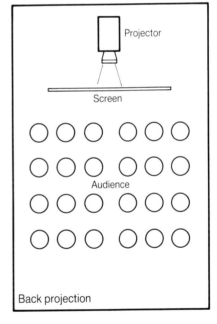

Front and back projection

Slides are usually 35 mm in size but vary in the thickness of the board used to mount them (in Europe the board is thicker than that used in the USA). The slides are usually loaded into circular trays or carousels which can be fitted on to the top of the projector and hold 80 or 140 slides in slots. For small audiences, there are projectors which incorporate a built-in viewing screen and these would be suitable for 6–12 delegates, or possibly more if a high stand is used.

There are a number of aspects to bear in mind when designing slides and some of the points will apply to OHP acetates too.

Rudy Knight, author of *The Meeting Spectrum*, suggests that 35 mm slides are held at arms length against a strong light. If the copy can be read under these conditions it will be legible when projected. Other pointers to good design are:

• use the 5 x 5 rule: no more than five lines and five words per line

• use bright, vivid colours, not pastels; text reversed out of a background of black or dark blue is best, with effective text colours being white, yellow, orange or red

• letter height when projected should be 2.5 cm for every 7.5 m of distance between the screen and the back row of the audience

• making slides in horizontal format i.e. landscape rather than portrait will get over problems of visibility if screen is set low

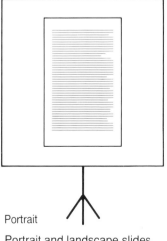
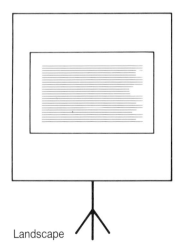

Portrait   Landscape

Portrait and landscape slides

- avoid long or full sentences on slides; use single words and phrases and distribute complex data as handouts
- use bold or extra bold sans-serif typefaces, in upper and lower case for legibility

THIS IS UPPER CASE

This is Upper and Lower case

This is a Serif face

This is a Sans Serif face

This is a Bold face

Examples of the best fonts to use on transparencies and slides

- make bold statements on slides, to gain attention
- to highlight one word or phrase in the copy run it in white, reversed out of black or dark blue, with all the other text in grey
- use charts and graphs, such as bar charts, pie charts, single-line graphs and multiple-line graphs

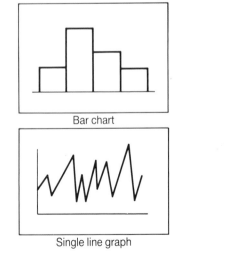

Bar chart

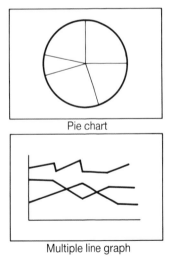

Pie chart

Single line graph

Multiple line graph

Examples of the types of charts and graphs to use

It is also worth noting that there are companies supplying standard slides on a variety of subjects and with a variety of graphic treatments. Also needed may be a number of 'spacer' slides to be used when the speaker has stopped showing a sequence of slides and is just talking. These can be logo slides carrying the conference logo (or trademark) or could be speaker slides showing the speaker's name and title/organisation.

'Off the shelf' slides are also available showing cups of coffee or a meal on a plate, an appropriate reminder of the time for both speakers and delegates. 'Welcome back' slides can add a nice touch.

Screens

Some thought will need to be given to the size and type of screen used, as well as its position in relation to the audience. Screens may be a fixture of a room or free standing and portable. A suitable wall can of course be used to project on to, and a whiteboard can also double as a screen. Manufactured screens can be either roll-up or fold-up versions.

For optimum viewing, the bottom of an image projected on to a screen or wall should be at least 2 m from the ground, unless raked (stepped) seating is provided. This is because delegates will need to see the image over the heads of delegates in front of them and most people are around 120–150 cm high when seated. Better viewing can be obtained by staggering the rows of delegates and/or placing the rows further apart.

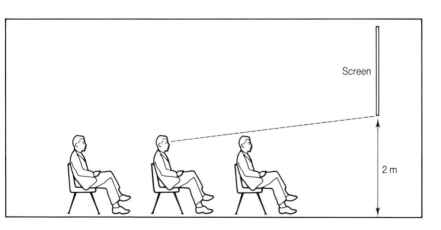

Optimum viewing height of the screen

The prospect of delegates having to see over each other's heads explains why large rooms with only 3–3.5 m high ceilings are unsuitable for audiences viewing any kind of screen.

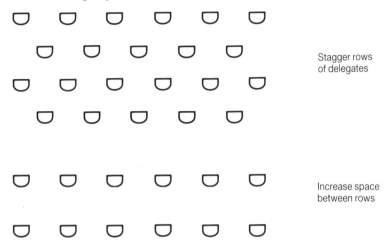

Stagger rows of delegates

Increase space between rows

The best layouts for optimum viewing

In terms of maximum closeness to screen and distance from it, it has been suggested that the 2/8 rule should apply, that is that no person should sit nearer than two times the height of the projected image, or further away than eight times. In terms of the angle to the screen, no

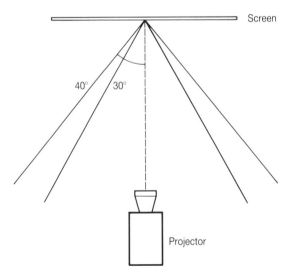

Optimum viewing angles from the screen

delegates should be placed at an angle of more than 40 degrees to the screen, or 30 degrees when it is a back-projected image.

It is worth bearing in mind, given the above, that the maximum number of delegates a venue states it can house theatre style in a room will not allow for back projection, which can cut a quarter or even a third off the totals. Indeed, the maximum numbers quoted by venues are not really accurate when using any sort of AV and this will need to be taken into account.

Video

If moving pictures are required, then video is usually the favoured choice over film, which is less convenient to show and more expensive to buy. Video quality is constantly improving and more and more venues are installing permanent facilities to play video tapes to large audiences, which is helpful as this is usually very expensive for an organiser to arrange.

For small audiences, a standard 95 cm (38 inch) (diagonal dimension of screen) TV monitor on a high stand will normally be adequate for an audience of up to 40. A good rule of thumb is around one delegate per inch, for example, a 43 cm (18 inch) monitor will be adequate for 20 viewers. Larger audiences can also be accommodated by installing more than one monitor and placing these strategically up the sides of the room on stands. Thus with six monitors of the 95 cm variety, an audience of 240 can all view comfortably. There are also large screen video units that use mirrors to 'fold' the image and back project it on to a built-in screen, but the picture quality of these is still fairly poor.

Organisers using video should be aware that there are three formats available: VHS, Betamax and U-Matic. For most commercial use, VHS is the main choice since it can be played on a variety of widely available equipment. There are also three standards of VHS player which are PAL, NTSC and SECAM. PAL is the standard used in the UK, most of Europe and Africa, Australia and South-East Asia. NTSC is the North American standard. SECAM is the standard used in France, Russia and the Middle East. A PAL player will not play a tape designed for NTSC equipment, and so on as the standards are simply not compatible.

Video screen at the International Convention Centre, Birmingham (*Source*: ICC Birmingham)

Clearly, this is an aspect that needs to be considered if an event is being held outside the UK or if a speaker is bringing a video tape from the USA or France. Some modern players will play all three standards at the flick of a switch but these are not always easily available and would have to be specified. Another solution is to have the tape converted from one standard to another, although this can be expensive and the picture quality can suffer.

There are other uses of video that conference organisers can consider. For a large audience, the speakers can be filmed live and their performance projected on to a screen. The same system could be used with panellists and at question and answer sessions. It is worth bearing in mind however, that to film members of the audience will require strong lighting and whilst the performers on stage will be used to this, a delegate, and all the others sitting nearby, may not. Filming the audience rather than just the presenters throws up a number of technical problems as well as possibly inhibiting questions, and there may also be legal problems involved because if the result is to be used afterwards, the delegates' permission should be sought.

Another use of video is the transmission, on closed-circuit television (CCTV), of something happening outside the building. The Octagon Room at Sheffield University has hosted medical conferences where actual operations taking place in a nearby hospital have been shown to delegates.

Finally, as with slides, there are a number of companies which now supply short, standard video clips to be used in a variety of standard sitautions, such as at the opening of a conference, or for calling a break etc. Some are humorous and others very dramatic. One UK conference organiser started his event with a video clip of Concorde taking off. However, after this, his own otherwise excellent presentation was something of an anti-climax.

Video is a powerful medium and needs to be used with care.

Other visual equipment

Another type of projector currently making a comeback at conferences is the real-image projector which projects an image of print, graphics or even an object up on to a screen. Text and pictures do not need to be first copied on to clear acetate, as is the case of an OHP. A book can be laid down open on top of the projector and the image of the page appears on the screen. A sophisticated version of this using cameras to film the object and project it is also on the market .

Data projection equipment whereby data stored in a computer can be projected onto a screen is also available, as an alternative to the simpler OHP arrangement already described (see page 86).

For pure entertainment and impact, laser shows, set to music, are also an option. The conference theme or logo can be rendered in laser-generated light. There is also, of course, a wide variety of special effects using dry ice for smoke and indoor fireworks (pyrotechnics).

More fundamentally, the lighting of the large event is something that will need to be considered, especially as most hotel venues will have lighting of the function room, rather than conference room variety. This is a job for a specialist and the organiser would do well to leave it that way.

As well as basic lighting for the speakers and panellists, there may be a requirement for moving spotlights, especially if a celebrity is appearing. Some stars of stage and screen have their own requirements in terms of strength, direction and colour of lighting. A number of useful special effects can be created by computer-driven lighting programmes.

Audio

This will generally encompass microphones and loudspeakers and, like lighting, is a specialist area.

Some events need no sound magnification at all and a good public speaker may well be able to project to large numbers of people without such artificial aids. Actors and actresses in theatres do it all the time. However, a hotel suite is not a theatre, with all the acoustical advantages and some speakers are quiet, so it is as well to have a knowledge of the various types of microphone available and their advantages and limitations.

Fixed microphones are those installed on a lectern or on an adjustable stand, and are ideal for situations where the speaker is going to speak from one point and wants both hands free.

For panel sessions, table mikes can be supplied on low table-top stands. Some speakers like to move around on stage and for these the hand-held mike with the trailing wire is one option. Better still is the lavalier mike which clips on to clothing or hangs around the neck and frees both hands.

Radio mikes allow total freedom of movement; the speaker can walk around the room, talk to individuals in the audience and be heard everywhere. Radio mikes can be attached to clothing, with the batteries stored in a separate unit which can be placed in a pocket. Some speakers, especially if they run impromtu interviews with delegates in the audience, will opt for the hand-held radio mike which can be passed around. These are also excellent for question and answer sessions where conference staff can pass them to delegates wishing to ask a question. If questions are encouraged then using such a microphone is the best way of getting them. If not, then the best deterrent is a single microphone

GENCO corporate announcement set showing fixed microphones (*Source*: Imagination Ltd)

mounted on a stand near to the stage; delegates instructed to approach it and give their name may think twice before asking their question. Most will opt to stay in the safety of their seat! A hand-held radio mike is also perfect for panel sessions where it can be passed between the panellists.

Radio mikes however do have their limitations. Metal objects in the room can interfere with transmission and local taxi-cabs may be using the same frequency, with distracting, if sometimes amusing, results. The batteries run down quickly and most AV companies would recommend putting new ones in for the morning session and then replacing them at lunchtime as a matter of course. Finally, speakers must remember, if they are wearing a clip-on version, to switch it off when leaving the conference room. It is said that the newsreader, the late Reginald Bosanquet, after finishing a session at the Wembley Conference Centre, went straight to the men's room to perform some noisy ablutions, fogetting to switch off his radio mike. The resultant noises caused much hilarity amongst the audience but were less amusing to the next speaker, who had already started, and to the conference organiser who was running all over the centre trying to find out which toilet Mr Bosanquet had entered.

As well as avoiding this obvious error, speakers should be briefed on microphone technique generally. Positioning is important and depends on whether the mike is unidirectional, meaning that it only picks up sound in one direction, or multi- or omnidirectional and picks up sound from all directions. Lectern, standing and table mikes are generally unidirectional. The right position for a lavalier mike is to hang it midway between the chin and waist. Other mikes should be positioned about 15 cm in front of the speaker's mouth but 5 cm below it for best results, though this can be adjusted for the speaker's natural volume. Speakers should not fiddle with mikes nor, when using a fixed mike, should they turn away whilst speaking, a common error easily committed when turning around to glance at a screen to talk about the slide being shown.

One word of warning about using microphones, especially the multidirectional ones; they will often produce a high-pitched squeal (feedback) if they are used too close to a loudspeaker.

As Barbara Nicholls in the book *Professional Meeting Management* suggests, if the sessions are being recorded, a back-up microphone should be used, preferably clipped to the same stand.

Many venues offer a built-in sound system. The Church House Conference Centre in Westminster has a circular meeting room with fixed seating and built-in mikes by every seat for speeches by the delegates and question and answer sessions. Hotels often have simple systems installed in conference suites which are fine for ordinary speaking.

Those wanting something better, for amplified music for instance, will need to bring in their own equipment, a course of action favoured by most production companies.

Other AV equipment

There are a number of other items that usually come under the heading of audiovisual equipment. Many events use a conference set, an arrangement of portable panels, often incorporating a screen for back-projection, which provides a backdrop to the event as well as providing something to hide all the equipment behind. The set can carry the conference logo and can be mounted on staging, and some advanced versions incorporate electrically-operated screens which can move into place for back or front projection. Speaker support items include lecterns, speaker prompt systems (Autocue), speaker communication systems and laser pointers. Lecterns can be simple wooden structures that just hold notes or complex modern versions that have built-in microphones and controls for slide projectors, video projectors and conference room lighting.

A modern electronic lectern (*Source*: Acco-Rexels Ltd)

A traditional lectern (*Source*: Acco-Rexels Ltd)

Lecterns might also contain speaker communication systems which warn that time is running out. Some have a system of green, amber and red lights to do this and others might incorporate a timer. These are electronic substitutes for a member of the conference team standing at the back of the room holding up five fingers for 'five minutes left', two fingers for 'two minutes left' and drawing a single finger across the throat in the time-honoured and dramatic sign for 'time's up!' These signals actually work rather well, and there are also other signs for 'speed up', 'slow down', 'louder' and 'softer' which are in general use. Make sure however that any signs used are fully understood by everyone. At one event, one of the speakers mistook the 'slow-down' sign for a 'speed up' one and finished in a rush, 15 minutes early, leaving the organiser to fill the time somehow.

Speaker prompt systems, such as Autocue, if properly used, can help prevent this. The words of the speech are usually projected on to a sheet of glass which is mounted at eye-level in front of the speaker with the words, theoretically, unseen by the audience. In this way, the speaker can give the illusion of maintaining the important eye contact with the audience whilst still being able to read the speech.

Opinions as to the use of such equipment vary. Politicians are common users because they have to give a large number of speeches which have to be read verbatim in order to be able to correct misquotes, and which would be impossible to commit to memory. The same often applies to those appearing on TV. However, in the rather different world of conferences, some feel that the sheets of glass between the speakers and the audience set up an unnecessary barrier, and that because everyone in the audience knows the speech is being read out, this makes the performance look less spontaneous, and even insincere. Another problem emerged at an event, staged by the Forte-owned Cumberland Hotel in London to promote the opening of a new conference room, where the audience was amused by the sight of the banqueting manager going distinctly cross-eyed trying to focus on the Autocue.

The future of AV?

A number of recent developments in the conference market are worth special note.

'Live theatre' whereby actors and actresses mingle with delegates and stage carefully scripted and pre-arranged presentations is an intriguing creative tool. 'Spontaneous' interruptions can be carefully planned, for dramatic effect. At one event the 'waiters' suddenly burst into song, and at another, one of the company executives was 'arrested' by the 'police' and temporarily taken away. Such devices should, above all, increase understanding and retention of the message, as well as provide entertainment.

Keypads or electronic voting devices offer a new dimension to an event. Used by the delegates to vote on a particular issue, the results are instantly analysed by a computer and can then, with data projection equipment, be projected on to a screen for all to see.

Assuming the right questions are asked, some very valuable data can thus be instantly collected and presented in an entertaining and dramatic way.

Finally, reference must be made to teleconferencing. This enables individuals or groups to confer with each other without actually meeting. The simplest and cheapest method of doing this is by telephone and involves a group of individuals in different parts of the country, or the world, telephoning a number at a pre-arranged time and all being hooked up together. Thus 10 individuals in 10 different offices can hold a meeting by telephone, without the costs and stresses of travelling. With video-conferencing, individuals and groups travel to a nearby suitably-equipped venue and are filmed live, with the results being broadcast to all the other individuals and groups who have done likewise. Thus delegates and speakers from London can talk to delegates and speakers from New York, Tokyo and Sydney and vice versa without anyone leaving their own country.

Such systems as audio- and video-conferencing have some very clear and obvious advantages apart from the novelty aspect, especially for those involved in international events where delegates have to fly long distances. However, given the points made in Chapter Five, the electronic medium, whilst useful in some circumstances, is no substitute for face-to-face meetings, which are what most delegates will prefer.

Points for Discussion

1 What are the pros and cons of flip charts? OHP's?
2 Why are 35 mm slides so popular?
3 Design some slides depicting 'Welcome' 'Coffee Break' 'Lunch is served' 'Afternoon tea' and 'End'.
4 When looking at a conference room in which a range of AV equipment will be used, what will you be particularly concerned with?
5 If you were the AV manager of an event, how would you brief speakers using microphones?

CHAPTER NINE

ORGANISATION AND ADMINISTRATION

It has been calculated that to organise a conference for 200 people for two to three days is likely to take up to 250 hours or around six normal working weeks, even without counting the two or three 18-hour days which will be needed just prior to the event.

Having booked the venue, there will be contracts to check and sign, insurance to be taken out, menus to be agreed, accommodation to be fixed and all the work which is vital for the smooth running of the event on the day. At this point, most experienced organisers rely on comprehensive check-lists built up over the years of running events, to ensure that nothing is missed.

Contracts

Venue contracts are becoming an increasingly familiar feature of arranging events and the prudent organiser will want to read such documents carefully before making a final commitment. Clauses on prepayment and cancellation are especially important.

At the time of writing, some venues are demanding a substantial proportion of the total expected revenue, sometimes 100 per cent, as a prepayment or deposit. However, hotels are not immune from going into receivership and money paid as a deposit could easily be lost if this happened. One hotel near to Gatwick Airport, the Gatwick Wena, launched a 'club' for conference organisers whereby an annual payment of £10 000 secured a number of benefits such as discounted meetings room and bedroom rates when events were actually booked in. Most of the organisers attending the presentation were suspicious of what looked like a desperate measure to generate large amounts of cash quickly and it is thought that no one participated. A few months later, the hotel was placed in the hands of the Official Receiver.

The cancellation of an event by the organiser, for whatever reason, will usually attract penalty payments, which are commonly assessed on a sliding scale depending on how much prior notice of cancellation is given. This scale is based on the likelihood that the venue can be re-let for another event which is clearly a reasonable possibility if cancellation is made six months prior to the date, much less likely if the notice given is only six weeks. Like all things, the cancellation clause is generally negotiable and the penalties will often be waived if the organiser can offer an alternative date (i.e. if the cancellation is a postponement) or if other business is being conducted.

A reduction in the expected number of delegates is another area for both sides to consider, which is especially common at events where delegates have to pay to attend, such as a commerical seminar or social event. Venues may, not unnaturally, wish to set minimum numbers, with penalties if the space and bedrooms booked are not taken.

Cancellation is sometimes made by the venue rather than the organiser and where this would result in losses, organisers should demand that such an eventuality is covered by the contract, or by a separate agreement. Organisers have had their events cancelled because a decision to refurbish a venue was taken after the booking was made or because a 'better' or more profitable event was found by the venue. Double-booking errors are common where staff turnover is high.

Insurance

Insurance against disasters is essential and the wise organiser will protect the event against the possibility of accident and injury of any of the participants (public liability) as well as against unforeseen cancellation, which would result in financial penalties being paid to the venue, the speakers and the contractors as well as the loss of any expected delegate income. Insurance should also cover the failure of speakers to show up, damage to the venue, and loss of delegates' or organisers' property due to fire or theft etc. At one sales conference, held by clothing company Timberland in 1993 at the Frimley Hall Hotel in Camberley, over £10 000 worth of sample jackets was stolen by thieves who entered through a fire door while the delegates were having dinner. A few weeks later, at the Pennyhill Park Hotel in Bagshot, the electronics company Sanyo had £130 000 worth of products stolen, much of it pre-production models being demonstrated to retailers. In both these cases, the total loss, in terms of the purpose of the meeting and the sales opportunities lost, was far in excess of the value of the items taken.

A good insurance broker specialising in events will be able to advise on the full risks and what the minimum cover should be. Those organising events in Europe and selling an inclusive package of accommodation and travel will need to comply with the EC Package Travel Directive, which may require taking out additional insurance.

Food selection

The selection of food for a conference is dealt with in Chapter Seven. Fixed menus are usually suggested by the venue and it is up to the organiser to specify what is required, should the menus offered be unsuitable. It is becoming more common, particularly for large residential events which include a gala dinner, for organisers to open discussions with the venue chef, and to attend a sampling of the dishes selected, perhaps accompanied by others from the organisation to give a selection of views.

Delegate accommodation

With regard to booking accommodation for individual delegates, the advice given by most organisers is simply, 'don't'.

The company sales or management conference, where all the delegates are attending free of charge, is, of course, relatively straightforward since there will be just one block booking with the hotel for a set and known number. Where, however, delegates have to pay their own hotel bill, there is the potential for hours of work on the part of the organiser answering individual and time-consuming queries on such things as car parks, check-in and check-out times, smoking and no-smoking rooms, pre- and post-conference accommodation, arrangements for partners and children, and a host of other details. It is always better to get such work done by the venue, which has specialist staff on hand to deal with it, or by a hotel booking agency. Some convention and visitors' bureaux may offer this service free.

Organisers will, of course, need to book their own rooms as well as any required for VIPs, speakers, contractors and others working at the event.

Generally, where delegates are to book their own accommodation, the organiser will book a block of rooms in anticipation of the take-up by delegates. This is usually at a negotiated price for the event and a date is set – the cut-off date – by which delegates have to book to get the special rate. A venue with accommodation will measure its turnover in 'room-nights', and any turnover figure required to secure the special rate, or to enjoy an even better rate, is usually expressed in this way.

Delegate travel

Once again, the process of booking is best done by experts with the knowledge and the staff to handle it. Special rates on railways, long-distance coaches and taxis might be arranged for a UK conference. For an international event, arranging an 'official carrier', an airline giving special rates to delegates in return for free publicity and a good take up of the option, might be possible.

Transportation at the event may also need to be arranged with a local company if courtesy coaches are needed to carry delegates between the hotels and conference venue, as well as out to social events and 'dine-around' restaurants (see Chapter Seven).

Registration forms

For many events delegates will have to complete a registration form and it is well worth thinking these through carefully to ensure that administration procedures are made easier for the organiser.

Some organisers insist that forms are typed, to ensure that staff don't have to decipher illegible handwriting with all the potential for errors which might ensue. Others specify that block capitals must be used, and encourage this by boxing or perhaps even better, part-boxing the lines to be filled in, as below.

Name

Name
for badge

Job title

Organisation

An example of a basic registration form using half-boxed lines

Certainly, the registration form should allow delegates plenty of space to write the required information and should only ask for what is absolutely essential. Other information, such as dietary requirements, views on issues to be discussed etc. are better canvassed when the letter of confirmation is sent. Delegates should be encouraged to take and keep a photocopy of their form for reference. Hotel and travel booking forms, if relevant, should be separate from the registration form.

The full name of the delegate should be asked for i.e. 'Mary Johnson' rather than 'Miss M Johnson'. Many women are not happy about announcing their marital status with a 'Mrs' or 'Miss' and some find 'Ms' even worse. The safest option is to ask for the names of delegates as they would like to see them on their badges, although even this enlightened approach is not without its problems. Is 'Pat Smith' a Patricia or a Patrick? Similarly, 'Viv Turner' could be a Vivienne or a Vivian. This is a serious problem if delegates are being asked to double up in rooms. The terms 'first name' and 'family name' should be used in preference to 'Christian name', which may well offend delegates from Islamic countries, and 'surname', which some overseas delegates will simply not understand. The term 'organisation' is better than 'company', which may be an inaccurate description.

Telephone numbers and fax numbers should always be asked for; it will save time and money if delegates have to be contacted quickly because of queries about registration or changes in the programme.

Organisers should test the registration form by filling one in themselves. Receipt of the registration form will usually prompt a confirmation letter, an invoice if appropriate and, perhaps a few weeks before the event, 'joining instructions' laying out all the information delegates will need to be able to attend and check in.

Badges

A small fortune awaits the person who can design the perfect conference badge, since most are compromises. Stick-on paper or fabric badges are fine for short sessions – up to one day – but not for longer events, as the adhesive wears off and can also mark or damage some fabrics.

The same criticism applies to pin-on or clip-on badges which can ruin fine silks, suedes and velvets. The badges designed to be slipped into a top pocket are fine but only for those with top pockets, and badges worn on a card around the neck can bounce around when the delegate is walking and can turn over thus losing their effectivensss. Probably the most popular badge at the moment is the clip-on version which incorporates a swivelling clip that can be applied from any angle.

Whatever method of attachment is chosen, it is important that the card containing the delegate's details is securely fastened as badges often signify that the delegate has the authority to attend sessions and functions, and in these circumstances, lost badge inserts can create enormous difficulties. A large clear-plastic holder which completely encloses the printed insert slipped into a slit in the top is probably the safest and best. At some events, the insert may need to be easily removable so that an imprint can be taken, or a bar-code 'swiped' (read).

Experienced organisers never send badges to delegates – too many get lost or left at home – but make them available for collection at the registration desk.

As well as identifying delegates for the benefit of the organiser and venue, badges fulfil a most important function for the delegates as they facilitate introductions and networking. In the USA, the nickname of the delegate may be included on the badge along with the state or country from which they come and this information can act as a conversation opener and ice-breaker.

Remembering how highly delegates themselves rate this networking, the badge starts to assume a significant importance in the scheme of things. For this reason, it is important that the names of the delegates and perhaps their organisations can be easily read. Clarity at 2 m is worth aiming for, especially as some delegates may be slightly short-sighted and may feel rather self-conscious peering intently at the small type on a badge pinned to someone else's chest; more so if the peerer is a man and the other delegate a woman. Misunderstandings can and do occur!

Type size should be around twice as large as normal typewritten text, and many of the dedicated badgemaking systems and computer software programmes that can be bought will allow for this. Printers can be programmed to produce larger type and some of the old typewriters can be adapted. Another easy and cheap method, especially for small numbers is to mark off an A5 sheet of paper in eight rectangles, type the delegates' names etc. in normal-sized bold type and then photocopy the sheet on to A4 card or paper labels, blowing it up to fit. This method gives large readable type for small numbers without specialised equipment.

Name	Name
Position	Position
Company	Company

1. Type 8 on A5 sheet
2. Enlarge to A4 size on copier and cut out

One quick and easy method of making badge inserts

Another way to get a particularly good-looking result is to have the badges hand lettered by a calligrapher which might not be too expensive a method in comparison with the other options. Some delegates, however, may find a stylised script hard to read.

A method of identifying different types of attendee might be needed as these could include delegates, speakers, organisers, the chairman, board and committee members, exhibitors, overseas visitors, members and associate members, students and companions, depending on the type of event. This can be done by printing on to different coloured insert papers, printing or writing in different colours, attaching coloured stickers or hanging printed ribbons from the badge, as shown on the cover of this book. Ribbons are popular because they look impressive and because a delegate may fall into two of the categories, for example, they could be a speaker *and* an overseas visitor a fact which could easily be identified using two ribbons. At some events colour codes or other markings might also be used to designate a delegate attending on just one of the days, or on all three.

In the area of security, chemistry has come to the aid of the organiser in the form of time-sensitive badges. These are printed with a delegate's name and incorporate a chemically-treated strip covered with release paper. When the paper is removed the strip gradually changes colour, or shows the word 'VOID' after a set period. High security events might also use photo-badges with a picture of the delegate. Another security idea comes from one American organiser who applies plastic medical wristbands to his contractors, a different colour for each day. These, once on, can only be removed by being cut off, preventing them being used unauthorised by anyone else.

One small but welcome trend is towards the re-cycling of badges by providing a box or bin for delegates to deposit their badges in at the end of the event. Not only is this environmentally friendly but it can also save a considerable amount of money at future events.

In general, most delegates like wearing badges, accepting that a large part of the value of the event is the networking, made easier by good badges. Indeed in the USA, many delegates wear them with pride, a contrast to the surly British delegate attending a function in the media industry who was heard to growl, 'I don't wear a label. If people don't know who I am they are not worth talking to.'

Fortunately such posturings are rare.

Delegate lists

Delegate lists are often the subject of heated debate. If an exhibition is supporting or running alongside a conference, then exhibitors, who may have paid considerable sums to attend, will usually expect to be supplied with a list of delegates' names, addresses and telephone numbers, for follow-up in the future.

Delegates attending the conference may also value such a delegate list, perhaps for the same reasons. Those delegates with something to sell will doubtless be pleased to receive the names and addresses of potential customers but the potential customer may, understandably perhaps, feel rather differently and these views must be respected. This does not apply of course, to events such as sales conferences put on by individual companies for their own staff.

The organiser of a successful event attracting paying delegates wants the delegates to know who else is there because it encourages networking, and the list, if it represents a valuable cross-section of well-regarded individuals in an industry or profession, will elevate the event in the eyes of all the attendees.

One solution is to simply publish the name, along with the job title and organisation to which the individual belongs, if appropriate. In this way sellers can still network and buyers don't have to give out their addresses, unless they wish to; they will not be exposed to direct mail or tele-marketing campaigns afterwards either.

Signposting

Signposting at the venue needs to be carefully thought out beforehand, not hastily erected on the day. The venue will usually have a board listing the function rooms and events occupying them but organisers might prefer, if the event is large enough, to have their own personalised signs made. These can be as large and expensive as semi-permanent signs and banners hung outside the venue, or as low-cost as directional signs made on a photocopier with the front cover of the conference programme or logo and a pointing finger symbol.

Other types of sign needed may be:

- signs denoting session subjects placed at the entrance to the room

- name boards for panellists

- signs designating 'No Smoking', 'Reserved' (for back rows of seats), 'No Entry', 'Meeting in progress' etc.

- signs over registration with the name of the event

- signs at the registration desk indicating where to queue i.e. 'Pre-registered delegates', 'On-site Registration', and 'A–K' and 'L–Z' designations

It is important to have such registration area signs erected *over* the area and not mounted on the front of the desk where they will be obscured. This will irritate delegates who may have to queue up again if they inadvertently join the wrong line.

Other signs might denote 'Organiser's Office', 'Press Room', 'Speakers' Room', 'Overseas Delegates' Lounge' and so on. Signs can be made professionally using film die-cut by computer-driven cutters of the type used by most exhibition contractors for fascia boards, or they can be produced by a studio with rub-down or hand-drawn lettering.

Registration

This too needs to be planned well in advance. The registration area will need to be large enough to accommodate storage of materials and stations for all necessary staff. As a general guide, if delegates are pre-registered and merely need to queue to collect their badges, documents and delegate packs, then one member of staff should be able to handle 100 delegates per hour. If delegates have to be registered on-site, however, this can drop to 20 or less per hour. Clearly, the more who pre-register the better. For on-site registration, it is a good idea to have booths set away from the main queues where delegates can stand and fill in their details on a special registration form. Alternatively, they could present registration staff with a business card clipped to a form to save time.

The handling of badges and delegate packs at registration needs some consideration. Ideally, delegate packs should not be personalised with the delegate's name since this entails the physically ardous job of sifting through many to find the right one each time a delegate registers. A better system is to keep the packs all the same and just hand one out with each badge. Badges are easier to handle if they are placed in envelopes with other relevant documents (meal vouchers, invoice copies etc.) with the name of the delegate printed on the outside top of the envelope. Any special instructions, such as 'bringing cheque or cash' can be written here too and the envelopes stored upright in a box or slotted rack for easy access. Badges laid out on tables are not the best method as unprincipled delegates can help themselves to someone else's badge. Badge envelopes can be placed in alphabetical order of the delegates' last names – the most common system – or by organisation, a time-saving method if a number of attendees from one organisation all arrive together.

A registration desk (*Source*: Apollo Photographers Ltd)

Registration staff, whether employees, volunteers or from an agency will, of course, be carefully selected for their pleasing manner and saintly patience! Nevertheless, it is good policy to have one senior member handle all queries and problems. There will always be lost badges, new badges to make on the day, delegates who think they have paid but of whom no record exists, journalists who turn up unannounced and expect a free place, overseas delegates who need a little extra help and so on. Queuing will be speeded up if such problems can be quickly diverted away to someone specially briefed to deal with them.

A number of agencies exist who supply registration staff, and some are better than others. It is not a job for someone more used to looking glamorous on an exhibition stand. On the broader issue of appearance, most organisers will see the sense in only using welcoming, friendly-looking staff, and it is, perhaps, a good idea to dress them in the conference colours. It is obviously better to have too many registration staff than too few.

On-site operations at the event itself will be made far easier if detailed plans are made and contingency measures agreed on. Some major areas include the build-up, the conference office, handling of information, problem-solving and dealing with venue staff, and these are now discussed more fully.

The build-up

For many organisers, this is the bit that really gets the adrenalin flowing. It is usually a chance to put on comfortable old clothes, be treated like royalty by venue staff, enjoy some good food and drink and make hundreds of important decisions. It is the few hours when months of planning, scheming and working all come together.

Most organisers will first want to set up the conference office. This is the nerve-centre for operations and will commonly contain desks, chairs, word processors, computers, coffee-machines, photocopiers, fax-machines, telephones and staff.

As things start to click into place, the pace increases. The production team arrives and sets up the AV equipment. The delegate packs may need to be made up and perhaps stuffed with some commercial brochures, which are already waiting at the venue. The abstracts have just been delivered and need unpacking and placing at registation, which hasn't been set up yet either. Six more delegates have registered and need badges making up, four have cancelled, two members of the registration team have reported sick, a key speaker telephones to ask if he can bring his friend at no extra charge, and the AV team want to know where they can get a hamburger!

The good organiser anticipates. Even if the joining instructions state that check-in is from 9.00 a.m. to 9.30 a.m. some delegates will arrive, especially the ones who are registering on-site, at 8.00 a.m., and someone has to be on registration to sort them out. The AV equipment will need to be finally checked and if there is to be no on-site engineer all day, an emergency number should be obtained.

On the day

It is 9.00 a.m. and there is a growing hubbub filling the registration area as delegates start to check in. Tea and coffee have been available since 8.00 a.m. The queues are lengthening, and delegate packs are taken from behind registration and given to pre-registered delegates as they wait in line, to give them something to read. Finally, all but the last few stragglers are in the conference room, and the organiser breathes a sigh of relief. There are just a few more things to attend to ...

Message and information handling

If there is one consistent complaint about venues from organisers it is the way delegates' messages are handled. Nothing is more irritating to a delegate than to be telephoned during or after the conference by a caller whose original message was not passed on. Organisers must insist that there is a procedure laid down whereby callers are passed immediately to a member of the registration staff who can take the message and pass it on. Some organisers and venues use a message-board placed just outside the conference room which has the messages in envelopes pinned to it.

A notice-board can also be put up, and used for announcements of interest to all delegates, such as changes and additions to the programme. Some organisers even issue delegates with postcards and encourage them to advertise items for sale, situations wanted and vacant, holiday homes to let etc. a feature that again helps networking.

Problem-solving and troubleshooting

It is the ability to troubleshoot and problem-solve which sorts out the experienced from the inexperienced, but even the best can be caught out. At one US conference, notes Sara Torrence in her excellent book *How to run Scientific Conferences and Meetings*, an outside telephone line was connected to the conference office. At night this was locked yet several lengthy late-night calls were made to a number in Caracas, Venezuela. The organisers refused to pay for the calls saying that they must have been made by hotel staff. They may or may not have been but if the organiser had thought ahead and instructed the switchboard to cut the line off after working hours, or had unplugged the telephone and stored it away, the situation would not have arisen.

The dark side of organising a conference is that delegates can actually be responsible for considerable damage to the venue: tales abound of sales representatives in particular getting drunk and creating a nuisance. In *Successful Conferences and Meetings*, Leonard and Zeace Nadler note the case of the delegates attending a conference at a ski-resort. Some of the delegates, who did not ski, nevertheless knew what *après-ski* was all about and accordingly drank too much. When the real skiers returned, they were bombarded with empty bottles and ashtrays and counter-attacked with poles, snow and anything else that came to hand. The cost of the damage amounted to nearly £10 000.

Drink is the cause of much trouble at events and may even have more serious legal implications than the above (see Chapter Seven).

Other problems may involve the venue staff. The usual advice when a problem with service occurs is to report it to the venue conference coordinator or someone in authority. Organisers have had better results however, by disregarding this doubtless excellent advice and making their dissatisfaction known to the employee concerned, making it clear that, assuming there will be no repetition of the incident, it would go no further. It has been noted that staff, grateful not to be reported, have then been noticeably eager to please.

A further extension of this concept can be applied to the vexing subject of tipping. American organiser Larry Wilson, when running an event in a hotel, gives the doorman $100 on arrival, with the promise of another $200 if delegates are not expected to tip but still receive excellent service. Needless to say they invariably do.

Other problems that can test an organiser's mettle are malfunctioning air-conditioning, heating or audiovisual equipment, lost material, delayed speakers, bad weather which stops delegates attending, demonstrations and medical or fire emergencies. Contingency measures for some of these will need to be thought out.

Finally, a small but important detail; clear all documentation from the meetings room before leaving. At one UK conference, a competitor who called in after the event was rewarded with a full breakdown of the advertising and promotions budget left on a flip chart.

So it's all over now, or is it? Are there speakers to write to and thank? Are there letters of thanks to be written to the venue, to the registration staff, to the sponsors? Is there an event evaluation form to be sent to the delegates, and the results monitored? Is there a report on the event to be prepared?

And are you ready for the next one...?

Points for Discussion

1 List the things that could go wrong with an event. How many of these could be covered by insurance?
2 How do others like to be addressed? Ask 20 people how they would like their name to be shown on a delegate badge for an event.
3 Why are badges so important at events?
4 Think of an event for 200 at a venue you know. What signposts might be required for a two-day event with four plenary sessions and nine optional workshops?
5 How would you handle the question of delegate lists? Delegate messages?

CHAPTER TEN

RUNNING EVENTS FOR PROFIT

Many company events are not run to make money and delegates do not choose to attend but are instructed to go. At other events, such as company AGMs, press conferences, corporate hospitality and seminars that are held to sell, delegates are invited to attend free of charge.

It is, however, the event put on to make a profit with which we are now concerned. This involves adding another skill to an organiser's list of abilities: marketing.

In fact, it is likely that a conference or seminar staged for profit encompasses most of the business disciplines. A product (event) has to be conceived, designed, produced and sold at the right price, to the right market, using the right methods. These tasks are not for the faint-hearted. They can take vision, imagination, some courage and no little money, and the failure rate is high.

Even the experienced sometimes get it badly wrong. In 1990, a group of direct marketing gurus, all top speakers used to giving advice to others, formed 'The Marketing Academy' to present the ultimate direct-marketing course, based in a luxury five-star hotel on the Portuguese Algarve. Fees were around £2000 for a week and a programme of part-learning, part-holiday was offered. The project was aborted when no-one booked. One guru lost £55 000 of his own money and admitted, 'The proposition was wrong.'

More recently, in 1992/93, a conference industry magazine, *Meetings and Incentive Travel*, launched a series of seminars for conference organisers which was described as, 'The Definitive Development Programme for Event Organisers'. Two of the seminars were entitled 'Making Meetings Pay' and 'Marketing a Meeting' and included advice on how to attract maximum numbers of delegates. Sadly, the seminars were cancelled at short notice when less than four delegates booked places. Their own definitive advice, it seems, did not work for the organisers. As the magazine editor put it, 'Conferences for conference organisers are disasters looking for somewhere to happen.'

This said, many groups, such as associations and societies make a significant proportion of their income from events organised for their members. As well as an income, these events also provide an opportunity for officials to meet members and, despite recession, those commercial event organisers who can get the proposition, price and promotion right, can still succeed.

Choosing the subject and formulating the proposition is the first step. Generally, delegates pay to go to events if they feel one or more of the following will happen:

- they will update themselves on new developments, concepts or legislation

- they will learn something that will make or save them money

- they will therefore be able to do their job better

- through discussion they will be able to get more overviews and insights into their industry or profession

- they will meet their peers and increase their 'visibility'

- they will enjoy some debate

- they will be able to sell to the other delegates

- they will enjoy an expenses-paid break from routine

- the costs involved in attending and the time taken up will both be well worth the investment

Budgets

Having found a suitable subject for the market, the next stage is to work out a budget. This means listing all the costs: speakers, venue, AV equipment, administration and, most importantly, promotional costs. Then the likely income can be assessed and a break-even figure of delegates established. Below is a simple illustration of a possible budget for a one-day seminar.

Fixed costs

Speaker	£200
AV equipment	£200
Administration	£150
Promotion 5000 mailings @ 50p each	£2500
Design	£150
Contingency fund	£100
	£3300

Variable costs

Venue @ £25 per delegate

Income

£130 per delegate

Delegates	Income	Fixed costs	Variable costs	Total	Profit
20	2600	3300	500	3800	−1200
30	3900	3300	750	4050	− 150
40	5200	3300	1000	4300	900
50	6500	3300	1250	4550	1950
60	7800	3300	1500	4800	3000
70	9100	3300	1750	5050	4050
80	10400	3300	2000	5300	5100
90	11700	3300	2250	5550	6150
100	13000	3300	2500	5800	7200

Note that in the above example, the break-even point, where all costs are covered by income occurs between 31 and 32 delegates. It is also worth noting that, in terms of responses to mail shots, a 'low' is 0 per cent, and a number of promoters have mailed out 5000 brochures and got nothing. A 'high' is 2 or 3 per cent, with 0.5 per cent being very common. Thus, in the above example, unless the mailing-list is extremely select and responsive, the maximum response would probably be 100 delegates, a good result would be 50, and 25 would be very likely, so cutting the costs would be prudent. A smaller mailing to the best 1000 names might still produce 30 delegates at £130 (income £3900) with a fixed cost of only £1300 and variable costs of £750. Total costs would therefore be £2050 and a profit of £1850 would be made. In this instance, the break-even figure would be only 13 delegates. Cutting back elsewhere would reduce this still further. For example, with 30 delegates would you need any AV equipment?

Generally speaking, the lower the break-even number of delegates the safer and better. However, even if it is clear that the event will make a loss, it will still often be better to proceed once the promotion has been done. In the above example, if only 20 delegates actually book, it will certainly be better to run the event than cancel it. If cancelled, the bulk of the fixed costs will still have to be paid and the venue may also insist on a cancellation charge. Since the delegates will want their money back, the bill for cancelling could be around £3000, plus 20 disappointed delegates, plus the bad publicity. A £1200 loss, alongside this, doesn't seem so bad, plus, since smaller events are often more popular with delegates, some positive publicity could be gained.

The number of delegates, the main income factor, is so crucial to success that many experienced organisers decide how many delegates will book and at what price and then decide on the level of promotion.

Apart from the all-important promotion of the event, which is discussed later, there are a number of other factors which will affect the number of delegates who are likely to book.

Price

This is almost as important as the basic event idea. Some organisers have noted that a low price brings in junior delegates, a high price attracts the more senior. Others claim that the price should always be a little lower than delegates' expectations, which, incidentally, vary enormously. One organiser recalls, when charging £150 for a full-day

London based seminar, one delegate asking if it was, 'really any good at such a low price', and another asking what type of hotel accommodation it included. There is no real guide. At the time of writing, the half-day £50–60 session seems to be consistently successful, as does a £195 weekend course with two nights accommodation.

The question of what is included in the price is an interesting one. Some promoters include meals and overnight accommodation, arguing that people find it more convenient to buy a package. Others maintain that by excluding such items a lower, more attractive price can be offered.

The success, or otherwise, of a pricing policy will depend on the subject, the value to the delegates, the price charged by others, whether the individual or their organisation pays, the number of similar events available and the state of the economy.

Timing

An event that is a first of its kind always has the advantage over others that might follow. Sometimes a very fast response to proposed new legislation or to the outcome of a lawsuit can also be effective. Running a seminar alongside a relevant exhibition, with or without the blessing and cooperation of the organiser, has worked for some.

Regarding the programme timings, a city centre event might start at 10.00 a.m. to allow delegates time to get there, and conclude at 4.00 p.m., to allow delegates time to start for home, before the rush. The best days of the working week tend to be Tuesdays and Thursdays with Wednesdays, Fridays and Mondays following in order. Weekends are popular in some industries and professions, but very unpopular in others.

Generally, the months to avoid are December (because of Christmas lunches) and July/August with the proviso that very early July and very late August can be good choices since they avoid the bulk of the summer holiday period. If partners and even children are encouraged to accompany delegates then the 'summer school' concept can be successful.

Possibly the first rule of choosing the best date and time is that there are no hard and fast rules. One organiser runs a small London-based business event between Christmas and the New Year. Not everyone in business enjoys the long break and all the bonhomie, and the chance to slip away with a valid excuse and meet like-minded souls is, reportedly, an attraction.

Length

As a rule, shorter events pull in more delegates. One promoter claims a one-day session will 'out-pull' a two-day event by a factor of at least five to one. Certainly busy people appreciate a fast-paced programme that packs a lot in, and, in addition, the shorter event may not call for an expensive overnight stay.

Destination

For some UK organisers, London is the only city worth considering. One, running management events, estimates that a session in London pulling in 100 delegates will pull 15 in Birmingham, 20 in Manchester and 12 in Glasgow/Edinburgh. A lot will depend on the subject. A session designed for factory managers could do better in Birmingham than anywhere else, and a July/August event in Brighton, Bournemouth or Torquay, when it will be very cheap in the conference hotels, could also succeed, if delegates like the idea.

Venue

The actual venue chosen can affect numbers and a glance at Chapter Two will illustrate some of the factors. Some delegates will gladly throw themselves into the campus life of universities and others will only feel comfortable in four- or five-star hotels. Some will be attracted to the relaxed atmosphere of a country house or stately home property, others to a city centre hotel close to the nightlife.

Speakers

If the subject is one where there are known experts in the field then their names on the programme will usually pull in more delegates. The question is how many *extra* delegates will the 'star' pull in, and how much will it cost? This is especially true with speakers from overseas where fees, air-fares and London hotel bills could be from £1 500 to £5 000 or more. Organisers should calculate how many delegates' fees will be needed to cover the cost of the star and whether or not a lesser, but perhaps rising star, would represent better value.

The title

Some careful thought will be needed to devise a title which grabs the attention and starts the selling process. Some titles contain a promise of profit, examples of which would be 'Profitable mail order', 'The telemarketing goldmine' and 'Making money from meetings'. Others imply an educational result from attending, such as 'Successful negotiation', 'Dealing with the press' or 'How to design a brochure'. The promise of essential information is contained in such titles as, 'The EC Package Travel Directive – how it affects you', 'New developments in teleconferencing' and 'BS 5750 – some recent case-studies'. Sometimes the subject will be deliberately controversial and this flavour will permeate the title, as in: 'Conference organisers – are they good value for money?', 'The dubious ethics of corporate hospitality' and 'Advertorials in conference trade magazines – are they running out of puff?'

With the exception of the deliberately controversial however, titles should generally be positive and upbeat. 'Europe – a golden opportunity' might be better than 'Fighting the Euro-threat'. Also, people don't generally like being reminded how bad things are, as the author found out when only four delegates booked for 'Exhibiting through a recession', no doubt due to the recession!

The terms and conditions

Generally the policies of the organiser should make the event delegate-friendly. However, the aim is to make a profit and this can be eroded by a number of factors. If delegates book, are invoiced and then cancel, an administration cost will be incurred. Some organisers will allow this, some will insist that a booking is a booking and enforce it through the courts, and others will allow cancellation with no penalty in circumstances such as ill-health. Another approach is to allow cancellations without penalty up to a specified cut-off date, after which a charge is made. Some delegates may simply be able to send someone else to take their place and this should be encouraged. On such issues as cancellation, one promoter recommends that the rules be 'written tough but gently interpreted'.

Decisions will also need to be made with regards to whether or not to allow partners, and at what cost. Some allow partners to share rooms at residential events free of charge, letting the delegate pay the venue directly for any food and drink consumed by the partner. Others have a special partner rate and special events organised for them. Some care needs to be taken with the terminology used. Thirty years ago organisers would talk about 'wives' attending, but as more women moved into senior positions in business and the professions this switched to 'spouses'. As more and more couples choose not to marry, this has evolved to 'partners', and increasingly, the even safer 'accompanying persons' is used which, whilst twee, covers all possibilities.

On the question of credit control, it is considered by many organisers that money for events should always be paid beforehand, given the potential difficulties of collecting it afterwards. For some events however, this policy is not always possible for all the delegates and may depress bookings. It is something of a delicate balancing act to achieve customer care and judicious credit control.

Also into this category would come the issue of whether or not to accept credit or charge card payments. Most organisers, especially if selling events where individuals pay their own fees, have found that offering this facility can increase bookings. However, for the organiser this advantage must be balanced against the fact that a charge of around 2 per cent of the turnover, which could be 10 per cent or more of the profit, will be made by the card company.

Additionally, some charge card companies are not always quick to pay, increasing the cost to the organiser even further.

Promoting the event

Of all the factors affecting the delegate numbers, it is the promotion of the event that will generally have the greatest impact. Examples abound of wonderful events with superb speakers, staged in well-chosen venues which only pulled in a handful of attendees. The converse of this is that many poor or mediocre events, if they are properly marketed, can still make a substantial profit.

Assuming the proposition is right, then promotion is the process by which potential delegates are told about it. The main vehicle for this will be the brochure, suitably designed and produced and it is worth looking at this in some detail.

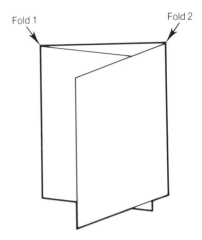

Fold 1   Fold 2

A two-fold brochure

The classic conference brochure for a one-day event is probably the two-fold variety as shown above. For longer events with lots of concurrent sessions a 16-page brochure might be needed.

The main elements are the title page, a description of the event, in terms of what delegates will gain (stressing the benefits of attending and perhaps describing the speakers) a programme and a registration form. This can be perforated to allow for easy detachment, or a scissor graphic can be printed on it, with a dotted line indicating where to cut.

Regarding the content and layout there are some points to bear in mind:

- stress the date and venue, mentioning them more than once

- stress the benefits of attending and spell them out: 'The coffee-breaks have been extended to 40 minutes to allow delegates time for the informal and spontaneous discussion of issues arising, which is such a vital benefit of attending.'

- repeat the logo as often as good design and taste allow

- give as much information about the event as possible

- personalise the approach, using words like 'you' and 'your' – a personal letter accompanying the brochure might also increase response

- for some events, photographs and biographies of the speakers are effective

- make it very easy for delegates to register by mail, fax or telephone. Ensure that the registration form is easy to fill in, and consider a separate registration form, where appropriate

- do not print information that the delegate will need on the back of the piece they return

- coated papers or boards are good to print on but difficult to write on; a matt surface is better

Above all it is worth remembering that designers are generally concerned with the overall look of a brochure rather than with its total impact on a potential delegate, its usability or, sadly in some cases, the practicality of printing it at a reasonable cost. An over-stylish and over-colourful design can actually depress response from some delegates, such as scientific or academic groups. Most are more likely to be influenced by the proposition than by the presentation. In terms of colour, it is probably better to stick to black and white, and perhaps a single red, blue or green for the logo, rather than go for full colour.

Perversely, a useful guide might be that if your designer hates it, run it. The author recalls attending a direct-mail 'clinic' in the late 80s when it was the fastest growing medium. A team of direct-mail experts was assembled and delegates brought in their direct-mail brochures for assessment. One seminar promoter sat through five minutes of hard criticism as the panel agreed that the one-day seminar brochure submitted, a simple creation in black and red which crammed eight pages of information into four, was totally lacking in any merit at all. Some of the remarks passed were, 'It's boring', 'The typography is out of the 60s', 'It's far too busy', 'No one's going to pay £150 on the strength of this' and, 'My first inclination is to bin it'. The chairman of the panel, whilst agreeing with the comments but not wishing to appear too unkind himself, asked the promoter, 'Have you had any response to this yet?' The promoter told him, 'Yes. I've had 470 paid bookings and there's still two months to go', a response which brought gales of laughter from an appreciative audience, and red faces to the critics.

This is not to say that, for promoting an event, brochure design does not have its place, but it may be considerably less important than the other elements. For good ideas on design, collect other organisers' brochures and adapt them to your own requirements.

Once design has been agreed then the brochure can be printed. It is worth considering carefully the size of the print run. Usually, it costs very little more to have 10 000 printed rather than 5 000 since the main fixed costs are in the platemaking and preparation rather than the variable ones of paper and machine time. Thus it would not be unusual to receive quotes for £1 500 for 5 000 copies and £1 900 for 10 000.

It ought to go without saying that the artwork, before going to the printer, should be carefully checked for errors. This cannot be stressed too much, and there are numerous examples of where an error, unobserved, has caused problems and embarrassment for organisers. Incorrect dates for events are an obvious error, but not so obvious is where the date is right but the day of the week given is not, i.e. showing it as 'Tuesday March 8' when March 8 is a Wednesday. Incorrect pricing can also cause problems, the '0' left off '£150' being an obvious example, but where Value Added Tax (VAT) is charged, errors in simple addition can occur, for example, 'Fee £165 plus VAT of £28.88 = £183.88'.

Simple typographical errors can also cause some unwanted embarrassment if not picked up and corrected. The giant US conference trade association Meetings Planners International (MPI) unintentionally amused potential speakers at its events when it announced a new mehtod of calling for papers. Unfortunatey, the news was actually announced as, 'A new method of culling innovative and creative presenters and speakers is being tried at MPI Headquarters.' In another case, an expensive reprint had to be made of brochures describing courses in English for overseas students, which were held in various UK towns and cities. Unfortunately, in the short description of Southampton it was claimed that the town was noted for its 'pubic gardens', hardly a good advertisement for an organisation selling its grasp of the English language to others.

Having produced a suitable brochure, the next stage will be to distribute it to as many potential delegates as possible. This is usually done by direct mail, but brochures can also be inserted in magazines or newspapers. Advertisements can also be taken out in these media to generate enquiries, and some may be persuaded to publish factual information about the event if sufficiently newsworthy.

Since the promotion of the event often represents the largest single cost, it is worth looking at the various methods in a little detail.

Direct mail

This is invariably the first choice of most organisers. If the proposition and brochure are right, the good mailing list is the essential third element on which success can be built.

Some organisers will already have good mailing lists, or access to them. For those trying to build good lists of names and addresses or needing to buy or rent them, some pointers will be helpful:

- Trade associations and societies, with members who are potential delegates, are excellent sources. Lists can be bought, or the brochure inserted in the newsletters or journals distributed by the association or society. A special discount for members will usually be highly effective and may also attract an editorial mention. There are a number of directories which list such associations.

- A list of members as above would be termed a response list in that to join, members had to demonstrate their interest by paying something. A simple list of say, architects or factory managers would be termed a compiled list and may not pull as well.

- The best response list of all for event organisers is a list of suitable people who have paid to attend another organiser's event. Thus, if it was desired to promote an event entitled, 'The impact of EC directive 38 on hotel banqueting managers', a compiled list of hotel banqueting managers would probably work very well. A response list however of hotel banqueting managers who had paid to attend such events as, 'Serving creative banquets', 'Saving fortunes on banqueting' and, 'The hotel banqueting manager's annual conference' would probably work even better. Some people just love going to events and organisers should always get to know other organisers and exchange lists, wherever possible.

- Those who have bought books, audiotapes or videos on a given subject would also be worth mailing. Such lists may be sold by the publishers of such items, or they might exchange them for a distribution of their own literature at the event.

- Lists on labels can cost anything from £50 per 1 000 to £500 per 1 000 with a commercial price of £150 – £250 being the norm.

- There are many poor lists being sold. One, supposedly of the UK's top 2 000 hotels, contained the names and addresses of boarding houses, cafés and even some Chinese restaurants. Always check a list before mailing from it and return it to the supplier if not suitable.

- Lists that do not include named individuals are often far less effective than those that do. It is pointless just addressing a mailing piece to 'Shell UK' or 'Forte Hotels'. If individual names are not available, then sometimes a job title can be effective, for example, 'The chief chemist', 'The sales director' or 'The travel manager'.

- Old lists are often a waste of money. It should be noted that lists of names and addresses of business executives in most industries degenerate by about 30 per cent every year, so on a list that was compiled a year ago, about a third of its names and addresses will be incorrect because individuals will have died or moved on, and companies will have been wound up or moved. On this basis, a two-year-old list will be almost worthless and a three-year-old one totally so. Consumer lists of householders are not subject to the same factors.

- Mailing the list is one way to keep it 'alive', that is to stimulate those on it to buy something, and also to 'clean' it, that is to identify all the 'gone-aways' where mailings are returned unopened and delete them. Enquiries should therefore be made as to how often the list is sold and when it was last mailed. List owners usually reimburse organisers for the 'gone-aways'.

- If a list is already known to be good for response then additional copies of the labels can usually be ordered for a significantly lower charge. A responsive list can be mailed more than once.

- Most list owners will sell a sample portion of a large list for testing. Take advantage of this, before buying the whole list.

It is essential that all the brochures sent out are coded in such a way that the response from each list, or test portion of list, can be measured. Only by doing this will organisers ever know which lists have worked.

Codings can be done in a number of ways. The simplest and cheapest way is to run a felt-tip pen down the side of a stack of brochures, so as to leave a small mark on the edge of the reservation form. By using different colour combinations and positions a variety of codes can be applied. If numbers of mailings are small then a small dot discreetly placed on the registration form can be hand-done at little cost. For large numbers of brochures the codings can be applied by the printer. Sequential numbering is another way and changing the copy in a minor way is yet another. It is worth knowing however that one of the best ways to code is to print a line of numbers, say 1–20 on the bottom of the registration form. A run, of say 10 000, can be made before the machine is stopped and the figure 20 etched off the printing plate with acid, (it is very difficult to add to a plate, very easy to erase). Another 10 000 can then be run which will show 19 as the last number, after which the 19 can be removed and another 10 000 run off, and so on. In this way, a total of 21 codes (some can have no numbers at all) can be easily and cheaply used.

An alternative to coding brochures is to have the address labels coded by the list owner, then applying the address labels to the registration form and inserting the brochure into a window envelope so that the name and address shows through. This method, whilst more satisfactory in many ways, may not be suitable if a large portion of the distribution is to be used as inserts in the trade or consumer media (see next section) or distributed at exhibitions or other events.

Inserts

Brochures can also be inserted in trade or consumer publications and for some events this can be highly effective. The brochures then get to the readership of the publication (the target audience), and the cost per brochure is usually far less than mailing, where the cost of the list, envelopes, labour and postage has to be taken into account. It is however, out of the organiser's control and problems have in the past arisen. Many trade magazines, whilst declaring their publication dates, regard these as something of a movable feast, depending on how much advertising has been received. Thus an organiser running an event on May 1 might book an insert in the March issue of a trade publication, expecting it to land on potential delegates' desks by March 12. The magazine meanwhile decides that, because of a lack of advertising, they will produce a combined March/April issue and that this will be posted on April 15. Given that many magazines use the cheapest postal service, copies may not reach readers until April 23/24. If opened and read straight away (how likely is this?) then with luck the organiser's event will be advertised to the reader just one week before it is due to happen.

Another problem with trade magazines is one of honesty. The claim might be that '10 500 copies are distributed'. The reality however, especially when times are hard and money is in short supply, is that only 4 000 are actually printed, and the bulk of the organiser's brochures are dumped. A magazine which is a member of the Audit Bureau of Circulation (ABC) is a safer bet than one that isn't but even this is no guarantee that the copies mailed are going to the right audience and many may go to potential advertisers.

Advertising

This is not generally an effective way of promoting events. Magazines are usually printed on coated stock which is unsuitable for the registration form. Few delegates will bother to cut a page from a publication to send a piece of it in as a registration anyway.

If advertising is used it should be of the 'telephone or fax for full details' variety, but inserts are usually better.

Telemarketing

In conjunction with direct mail and for small numbers this can be highly effective. Potential delegates can be mailed, then telephoned to get a commitment from them. A personal telephone call inviting delegates to attend can make them feel wanted, or hunted, depending on how well it is done.

Some organisers would advocate the phone/mail/phone sequence where an organisation is contacted to find out the names of likely delegates, who are told in outline about the event. Those expressing an interest are sent full details, and then telephoned again to secure a commitment.

Telemarketing is also a good way of 'cleaning' a list before mailing, checking that the individual is still in the position quoted on the list.

Editorial publicity

If a magazine or newspaper editor can be persuaded that the event will interest readers some valuable coverage may result. Many speakers have good editorial contacts and these can be used by the organiser. Press interviews with speakers can be carried out before the event, as can interviews for radio and TV.

Dealing with the press is a specialist area where, like in many other areas, experience is a great comfort. Some organisers will prefer to hire a PR specialist and if the budget permits this might be a sensible move. If not, there is no reason why an organiser cannot telephone the editors of relevant journals, or the specialist editors of newspapers, and, stating the subject of the event, sound out any interest. Alternatively a simple direct press release can be prepared and mailed.

Some editors may even want to attend the event, or send someone to cover it and this could be an extra bonus. Care, however, should be exercised with editors of trade magazines who will often distribute such press passes to adverising sales staff, who are only too pleased to have a hosted day out and a chance to sell to delegates. The organiser should make sure that only editorial staff attend,

Most magazines and journals publish a diary of forthcoming events and the compiler of this can be a useful contact.

Other ways to promote

Further use can be made of the mailing list with potential delegates being mailed 'updates' as the event draws nearer. These can be in the form of a letter or newsletter and might announce a new speaker who has just agreed to speak, a description of some of the commercial organisations attending the exhibiton or the support of a new sponsor. Also very effective is to send a list of organisations that have already booked delegate places.

To encourage bookings, delegates can be given a special discount for confirming by a set date, and discounts can also be given for block bookings of two or more delegates by the same organisation. Delegates confirming their booking can be offered a chance to bring a colleague at a lower price.

If a suitable trade journal or newspaper can be persuaded to sponsor the event, this can be very helpful from the point of view of the cheap publicity gained. In return, the journal could receive a payment based on the number of delegates booking. Some journals will be happy to get involved at the very early stages of planning and lend their name to the event, valuing the exposure this gives them.

It may be possible to find commercial sponsors who will pay for delegate wallets, pens, pencils, the coffee-breaks, the lunches or dinners and, if relevant, the courtesy buses, all for the appropriate recognition of course. Organisers can sell add-on items including tape recordings of the sessions, session papers, partner tours, social events as well as the delegate list (with addresses and telephone numbers) itself.

Lastly, organisers can, assuming the event attracts enough delegates of the right type, persuade commercial organisations to take exhibition space to sell their goods and services. On the plus side, an exhibiton can generate significant amounts of money (some even cover the whole cost of the conference) and give delegates something to look at during breaks. In addition, exhibitors can help promote the conference. On the minus side, they may, because they tie up extra space at the venue (and space that can't be used by the venue for evening functions), actually cost a lot money to put on.

Points for Discussion

1 You are running a one-day conference to make a profit. Your fixed costs are £4650 and your variable costs are £31 per delegate. At a fee of £165 per delegate how many delegates will you need to break even? To make a profit of more than £2000?

2 Think of a subject you would personally like to have covered by a seminar. How much would you pay? What month would you like it to be? What day of the week? How far would you travel to attend?

3 Think of some titles for sessions which would appeal to you for the seminar you decided on in Question 2.

4 Design a simple brochure for the seminar described in Question 2.

5 What are the main factors affecting the quality of a mailing list?

CHAPTER ELEVEN

OVERSEAS EVENTS

The organisation of events overseas represents an additional set of challenges to the conference organiser.

Aspects that will need to be considered are the logistics of getting to the destination as well as questions of culture, customs, food, climate (political as well as weather), currency and pre- and post-event activity.

The rewards however can be worth the trouble. Travel by air has never been easier or cheaper and the overdue breakdown of monopolies in the airline business can only increase competition and reduce costs still further. Resort hotels in many overseas locations fight very hard to attract conferences in their low seasons, often the prime time for such events anyway, and the attraction to delegates of flying away from the cold and damp of the UK in winter for a few days by a warm sunny beach cannot be overestimated. One organiser found in 1992 that it cost the same to hold a two-week winter seminar in a quiet resort hotel near Valencia, Spain, as it did in Manchester, even allowing for the air fares.

Some of the specialised aspects of running events overseas can, however, markedly increase problems and costs for organisers and each of these are discussed in turn.

Types of venue available

Serious business meetings and conferences may not be as important in other countries as they are in the UK or the USA, and the venues will reflect this. In Barcelona, many of the hotels are more geared up for weddings and social functions, and in Malta tourism is the main business. Organisers looking for a dedicated conference room and staff will need to bear this in mind.

The USA is particularly good for meetings and most hotels will have their own dedicated staff too. The visitors' and convention bureaux are efficient and helpful and will, given a brief, organise a string of inspections of venues and attractions in their areas. Hotels commonly do not charge for meetings rooms and, because of the policy of charging by the room rather than the guest, can be very good value for delegates 'twinning up' or bringing partners. Many have low-cost 24-hour fast-food franchises (Burger King, Pizza Hut etc.) on site.

Overall with overseas venues, it is worth noting that 'star' ratings vary from country to country; it is not uncommon for a five-star property in one country to equate to a three-star one elsewhere. Site and venue inspections are essential.

Costs

Overall costs of running an event overseas need to be carefully calculated. State taxes and service can add 30 per cent to a hotel bill in New York. Costs of audiovisual equipment are especially high in some countries. Also to be budgeted for are costs of translating contracts and money changing.

The cost of drinks in some countries is very high; a carbonated drink costing 30 pence in a UK supermarket costs £3 from the mini-bar of a city centre hotel in Norway and a pint of lager in a Dubai hotel is £4 (1992 prices).

Currency

Apart from the cost of changing currency, fluctuating exchange rates can play havoc with a fixed budget. Between booking the conference and actually running it, costs calculated on the exchange rate at the time of booking can rise or drop by up to 20 per cent or more, depending on the country (or even more in high inflation areas like South America). Most organisers, faced with such uncertainties, buy part, say 50 per cent, of their currency at the time of booking and take a chance on the other 50 per cent, exchanging it nearer the time. No money changing transactions should take place with hotels which will commonly charge a far higher rate than the banks for this service.

Air travel

The actual booking of an airline seats is something that most organisers will leave to a specialist travel agent.

It is worth noting however, that, depending on the size of group, the destination, the length of the trip, the time of year, the day of the week, the time of the day and the negotiating skills of the organiser, discounts on normal fares of up to 50 per cent can be obtained. Large groups can also charter their own planes.

Discounts are unlikely to be forthcoming when an airline has the only direct flight to a destination from the UK, and alternatives involving a change of plane may need to be examined. For example, the expensive way to Bermuda is to take the British Airways direct flight; the cheaper way, and one which opens up some useful pre- and post-event opportunities, is to fly to New York and then down to Bermuda.

As in negotiating with hotels, organisers may find it easier to agree non-price benefits. These could include:

- upgrades, subject to availability
- complimentary flights for staff (1 in 15?)
- use of club lounges at airports with free drinks, snacks, etc.
- special freight rates for conference materials
- special menus on flight
- customised items, such as headrest covers, eye-shields, etc.
- group welcome by captain on flight

The logistics of air travel will need to be carefully considered. Faced with delegates arriving from all parts of the UK to an airport for the outbound flight, many organisers will start the meeting at a nearby airport hotel, perhaps the night before flying. This means that people and their luggage can be coordinated and in some cases check-in can be made from the hotel, if this facility exists. Many hotels, near Heathrow airport for example, offer special low 'fly-away' rates for this purpose and will provide a courtesy bus to the airport.

Possible check-in problems should be anticipated, especially at busy times. The usual advice is to check in one hour before the flight leaves. At peak times this may not be enough time and airlines will not accept any responsibility for flights missed because of this, even if their own staff shortages have caused the problem.

It should not be assumed that tickets are always made out correctly, even when organised by a reputable travel agent. However, it may be some consolation to learn that even the experts get caught up in ticketing errors. At the annual conference of travel agents belonging to the Association of British Travel Agents (ABTA) a few years ago, some delegates flying to Acapulco and making several plane changes, found that they owned tickets for flights that didn't exist!

Many companies, especially if taking all their top executives or customers away, will think very carefully before booking them all on the same flight. Tragedies do happen and the prudent organiser may need to pause and think about the unthinkable. It is said that executives working for computer giant IBM will not only not fly together as a large group but will deliberately avoid taking the same lift. This may be apocryphal.

Flight times to a destination can cause some organisational problems. Flights into Rio from the UK arrive at around 6.00 a.m. after 10 or 11 hours flying. Those delegates unable to sleep on a plane, and many can't, will be very tired. Most hotels will not allow check-in to rooms until after 1.00 p.m., unless special arrangements are made, which usually involve money. Some organisers get around this by loading delegates onto a coach and taking them off for a gentle tour up the Corcovada mountain, to see the statue of Christ the Redeemer and the magnificient views of the city. Similar problems may be encountered when flying to India and South Africa.

Jet lag is something else to be considered and delegates unused to this particular joy of long-haul travel will need to be given some advice.

Flights to New York, for instance, leave London just before lunch UK time and arrive just after lunch, US time, after a seven hour flight. There is a five hour time difference between London and New York, that is they are five hours behind. Delegates will usually feel ready to sleep therefore at 7.00 p.m. New York time (their body clock says it is midnight). Those that do give in to sleep will be waking up at 2.00 a.m. (or 7.00 a.m. UK time), and will be wondering what to do in the five hours before breakfast. They will be yawning again by the early evening. It is better for delegates to force themselves to stay awake until 10.00 p.m., US time (3.00 a.m. UK time) on the day of arrival – a dinner at 8.00 p.m. can help – and then sleep a long nine or 10 hours until breakfast time. In this way a very quick adjustment to the time difference is made.

Flying west to east is usually worse. Popular flights from New York to London (the 'red-eyes') leave at 8.00 p.m. New York time. The flight takes seven hours and delegates arrive therefore when their body clock, now adjusted to New York time, tells them it is 3.00 a.m. and that they should be deep in sleep. Sadly it is not. It is 8.00 a.m. UK time and already the start of a new day. Organisers flying delegates in from North America in this way should not expect them to function efficiently on the day of arrival; around two full days are needed before most people get back to normal.

Delegates may also need advice on the dangers of excessive in-flight alcohol. At 30 000 feet alcohol is absorbed much quicker by the body and its dehydrating effect adds to the normal dehydration which is a part of a long flight. Thus is is not uncommon for delegates who overindulge to arrive at the conference with a massive and unpleasant hangover, not the best of starts. On a more serious note, those delegates returning to the UK often forget that their car is parked at the airport and take more drink than they normally would with their early morning 'dinner'.

Customs and Excise

The restrictions on duty-free goods such as tobacco and alcohol have all but disappeared for travellers within EC countries. However, there are still a number of restrictions in force dictating what can and can't be brought into the UK and organisers should note these and advise delegates. Also essential is some advice on what may be taken to other countries from the UK: a bag of apples once delayed a delegate for two hours at New York customs, and meat products can also cause problems. If travelling to Muslim countries it is advisable to check carefully all literature. The laws on the depiction of bare female flesh are extremely strict and even an advertisement in a newspaper or magazine showing a woman in a shower could cause offence and possible delays. In some areas of the former Eastern Bloc, ordinary Western magazines may be considered subversive, whereas pornography would be acceptable.

Drugs, that is 'hard' drugs, would earn your delegates the death penalty in some Asian countries, such as Thailand, and a long and very unpleasant prison sentence in Turkey. Even innocent but unthinking delegates can however fall foul of customs officials.

The author recalls the embarassment when a small polythene bag full of washing-powder was lifted out of his luggage by an unbelieving customs official in Dubai. Fortunately, it was easy to prove, by the application of water, that it was indeed washing powder and not some other substance. Such items, and pills as well, should be left in their original packets. Even here there are dangers: the analgesic substance codeine is banned in some countries.

Those carrying computers should be prepared to prove that they can be made to work; computers are apparently favoured receptacles for the smuggling of drugs.

Customs and culture

The culture and 'ways' of a country are other aspects with which delegates will want to be familiar. Some customs officials may even need to be bribed in order to get vital documents signed. There is no point in delegates taking a moral stand on this, as in some countries it is just normal practice, like tipping in the USA.

More fundamentally, however, the differences can have a substantial effect on the holding of an event. Jewish delegates would not be allowed to attend a conference in any of the Arab countries, and in those areas women would not be accorded the same equal respect as men. Drink is also banned in many Arab countries, with prison sentences for offenders. The attitude of some races towards work and commitments is markedly different to that in the USA and UK; in Mediterranean lands the '*mañana* syndrome' rules and strict timekeeping is often seen as unnecessary. This casual approach can be socially charming but frustrating if a schedule needs to be maintained. Organisers wanting a bus to arrive at 10.00 a.m. are advised to order it for 9.30 a.m., and then if it arrives on time, to apologise for their delegates' lateness. In South America, when a request from an organiser is answered with a 'No problem' it means simply that the recipient has understood the request. Whether or not it will be carried out is another issue entirely. An Arab would rather agree to do something and not do it than refuse a request from a guest; it is not a deliberate attempt to deceive, just another approach to courtesy. The British philosophy 'my word is my bond' is respected, but not emulated, all over the world.

Some other attitudes overseas genuinely disgust many in the UK. Those upset by overt racism might not wish to go to Africa, the Southern States of America, Arab countries or India. Our own attitude to and treatment of animals is generally different to that prevailing in, say Spain. The corrida or bullfight, much loved by the older generation of Spaniards, is something that, according to one travel agent specialising in Spain, 'might appeal to three or four out of a UK group of 40'. Clearly the organiser considering the inclusion of such an authentic taste of Spain in a programme should take this into account. In Malta, France and Spain many UK visitors are upset by the shooting of wild songbirds, many of which are on their way to the UK, for sport. The sight of trapped wild birds in cages in street markets has persuaded many to find an alternative destination for future trips.

Other aspects of which the organiser will need to be fully aware will include the different emphasis placed on meals and their timings. In Spain, for example, breakfast is very light, lunch is a heavier meal followed by a siesta. Drinks and snacks (*tapas*) are taken between 6.00 p.m. and 10.00 pm., when dinner is finally served. Social life then goes on till the small hours and those organisers wanting delegates to dine at 8.00 p.m. and get an early night might have problems. Given the late night aspect of Spanish life, those expecting hotel staff to be setting up rooms at 7.00 a.m. might also need to reconsider.

Food and drink

For many delegates, a large part of the fun of going overseas will be the different food and drink that can be tried out. For others, however, this can be an aspect that causes some anxiety.

Meat-and-three-veg types could feel deprived in France and Spain where few vegetables are served and vegetarians and vegans could feel especially discriminated against. Garlic and olive oil feature heavily in many Southern European dishes which is fine if delegates like such flavours, but can cause misery if they don't. Those preferring white to red meat will also have a miserable time in South America where beef and lamb feature strongly. In Brazil, pork is most commonly served as fat belly pork with beans and a lot of salt in the local *fejoida* dish, which is most native Brazilians' Saturday lunch treat but not necessarily to everyone's taste. On the other hand the serious carnivores will love the Brazilian barbecue restaurants where roast meats are brought round to diners on swords and the waiters only stop carving when asked to. Pork lovers will love Germany. Those who do not eat veal, however, may have to be a little selective in Germany and Austria where the beaten breadcrumbed and fried veal steak or Wiener schnitzel is a favourite dish, although these days it is more likely to be made of the much cheaper pork, especially in the tourist restaurants and hotels.

The eating habits of those in other countries can also be offensive to some; the passion of the French for very rare or raw meat, frogs' legs, snails (escargots) and horse meat; the Japanese consumption of live fish; the Koreans love of dog (chow) and so on. However unless there is some moral or religious reason why the foods cannot be eaten, there seems little reason why they should not at least be tried.

Some slightly offbeat delights falling in to this category might be sushi and sushimi (Japanese raw fish), Maltese octopus stew, roast octopus and Norwegian raw reindeer steak thinly sliced and marinated in sweet cider. Another treat in the Southern States of America is catfish, very common and cheap. In France, it is surprising to find how delicious croissants are when dunked in hot chocolate.

Chosen with care, local specialities can enhance an overseas event: a robust *coq-au-vin* or *soupe de poissons* in France, a selection of tasty

A selection of Chinese specialities (*Source*: ICC. Birmingham)

tapas and *tortilla* in Spain, real clam chowder in New England and so on. Coffee-breaks can be more fun with local pastries: Limburger tarts in Southern Holland, gateaux in Austria, *Kaiser-Kuchen* (cheese cake) in Bavaria.

If there is one other happy surprise regarding food, it is that a sandwich in the USA is a wonderfully overstuffed creation that is a main meal, not a light snack. Iced water also comes automatically with a meal; it doesn't have to be begged for as in the UK.

Drink, for those used to paying heavily-taxed UK prices, can be a joy overseas. Most other European countries along with the USA and Australia are major wine producers and local wines can be enjoyed for a fraction of the prices charged in the UK. In South America, a very good white rum spirit *cachaca* (pronounced kashassa) is made from sugar cane and is sold in Rio supermarkets for the equivalent of about 50 pence a bottle. It is all too easy and cheap for delegates to overindulge in Rio. On the other hand, one of the cost areas to watch is that of the price of bottled mineral water in Southern Europe, often more expensive than wine. Areas with tap water unfit to drink do rather well out of the tourists (see section on health).

Language

Fortunately for those in the UK, English is the main business language of Europe with German and French next.

However, with the simultaneous interpretation facilities available today, there is no reason why all delegates should not equally enjoy multilingual functions. Those organising international events where many nationalities are attending can cater for these with interpreters in soundproofed booths delivering interpretations of what speakers are saying through delegates' headphones. Another way to solve the problem is to have the speaker speaking in one language and have the text of the speech 'flashed' or 'rolled up' on the screen in others. Thus, with a large enough screen a speaker can be speaking in English and the text, assuming a copy of the speech is made available for prior translation, can be shown in French and German. Other options used have been to supply delegates with transcripts, in their own language, or audiotapes. A further alternative, sometimes called 'whispered' interpretation, is available for those gatherings where only one or two delegates need the service, and involves interpreters sitting behind or next to the delegates and whispering an interpretation.

Speakers being interpreted simultaneously will need to slow down their normal rate of speech and an adjustment of 10 per cent slower is usually suggested.

Where a large number of the audience, for instance the majority, speak a single different language to the speaker then 'consecutive' interpretation is used. This method involves the speaker delivering a sentence or phrase and then waiting whilst it is interpreted, a process that doubles the time taken for delivery. From the speaker's viewpoint it also takes some getting used to. The author remembers delivering a talk to 30 Russian delegates in such a way. At the end of the talk was a rather good business story. The aspect of delivering the punch-line and then waiting what seemed an eternity for the chuckles of approval was quite unnerving.

On that occasion the interpreter got every word right but organisers should be aware of the possibilities for error. Linguist Charles Berlitz notes the example of the French-speaking African delegate to the United Nations who wanted to say that some of the old tribal ways in his country had been abandoned and stated: 'Africa no longer erects altars to the gods' (*L'Afrique n'érige plus des autels aux dieux*). The interpreter, however, thinking that the word *autels* was hotels and that *aux dieux* was *odieux* translated the delegate's phrase as 'Africa no longer builds horrible hotels' (*L'Afrique n'érige plus des hotels odieux*). On another occasion the interpretation of a figure of speech caused problems when former Soviet Premier Nikita Khrushchev appeared on US television and the interviewer told him he was 'barking up the wrong tree'. The interpreter rendered this as 'baying like a hound' which, understandingly, did little for American/Soviet relations until a full explanation was given.

Some proverbs have almost equivalent translations, though shades of meaning can differ. The English proverb, 'While the cat's away the mice will play' is rendered in German as 'When the cat is out of the house the mice have a feast day'. In Mediterranean lands, the phrase becomes, perhaps, a comment on the work ethic. In Portugal it is, 'When the master goes out there is a holiday in the shop', and in Greece, 'When the boss is not around we know a lot of songs'!

Those organising events in the USA may feel that by doing this they are avoiding the language barrier, but this is not necessarily so. Lifts in US hotels are 'elevators', the taps are 'faucets', eggs are served 'over', 'over easy' or 'up' (fried eggs turned, or just fried on one side), the reception area is a 'lobby' and the porter a 'bell-captain'. Many other American words exist which mean something entirely different in British English, and delegates and organisers alike should be aware of the potential misunderstandings which can arise even when 'speaking the same language'. Body language too, especially gestures, needs to be carefully considered. The American 'OK' sign with a thumb and forginger means sexual intercourse in Brazil, as several organisers have found out to their cost and acute embarrasment! In Arab countries, the beckoning sign made with one hand is always made with the fingers pointing down, never up, and the thumbs-up gesture denoting 'I'm OK' in the UK is obscene in Australia, where hitch-hikers thumbing a lift simply extend a forefinger.

It is definitely worth finding out about any different social customs which if not followed can offend and possibly put delicate negotiations in jeopardy. For example, for many orientals, shaking hands is a dirty habit, and some races like more much more personal space between each other than others. In the USA, especially on the West Coast, full eye contact from male to male should be used sparingly in case a false impression is given. However, in South America, touching people when speaking to them usually implies nothing more than a desire to communicate, and in Arab countries, it is perfectly normal for two men to hold hands in friendliness.

Other considerations

Delegates travelling to overseas events may also need to be made aware of other potential problems. Physical danger may be one, particularly in the big cities of the USA and places like Kenya and Egypt where tourists have been killed. Certainly delegates need to know that walking around New York, Miami, Detroit or Washington late at night alone is far more dangerous than doing the same thing in London. Anyone going to Rio needs to be fully aware of the high crime rate and likelihood of being mugged.

Medical risks will also need to be considered and adequate time allowed for any necessary innoculations. Full medical insurance with an air-ambulance facility may be sensible for some countries. Even in the 'civilised' USA, victims of road accidents have been left bleeding while their insurance status has been checked, before treatment.

Delegates will also need to be given advice on healthy eating and drinking. In some Mediterranean areas, the seas are so heavily polluted that the consumption of mussels, which suck up the pollution, can lead to several days of misery. In many areas of the world, it is not advisable to drink the local tap water. However, thousands of people every year fall prey to bad stomachs because they forget that salads are washed in tap water and that ice-cubes are made of it.

Lastly, and a genuinely tragic sign of the times, in some areas AIDS is endemic. Whilst many organisers may not see themselves as guardians of their delegates' morals, few would be criticised for making those in their charge fully aware of the risks.

Points for Discussion

1 What might be the attractions to delegates of attending a conference overseas?
2 In which overseas destinations would you personally like to attend a conference, and why?
3 What special advice might delegates attending overseas conferences need to be given?
4 What cultural differences between the UK and other countries are likely to affect an event?
5 Should delegates be given the same sort of food and drink as they would enjoy at home, or the specialities of the country where the meeting is being held? Discuss.

BIBLIOGRAPHY

Berlitz, C (1983) *Native Tongues* Granada Publishing

Nadler, L and Z (1987) *The Comprehensive Guide to Successful Conferences and Meetings* Jossey Bass Inc.

Nichols, B (1986) *Professional Meeting Management* Professional Convention Management Association

Seekings, D (1992) *How to Organise Successful Conferences and Meetings* Kogan Page

Taylor, D (1988) *Hotel and Catering Sales* Heinemann Professional Publishing

Torrence, S R (1991) *How to Run Scientific and Technical Meetings* Van Nostrund Reinhold

Wright, R A (1988) *The Meeting Spectrum* Rockwood Enterprises

CONCLUSION

If, after reading this book, you get the impression that there is nothing really difficult about organising an event, that it just takes a logical mind, common sense, hard work and a little specialist know-how then you are about right.

As has been said, the business is simply a specialism although there are some further specialities within it for which further study may be needed. If you want to organise product launches then you will need to know about advanced audiovisual techniques, or know someone who does. If you want to make money from running commercial events then expertise in marketing aspects, particularly copywriting and direct mail promotion, will be most useful. In addition a good hands-on grasp of computer applications will definitely be an asset for those involved in the administration of any large gathering.

Beyond this, as in most other fields, personal experience is one of the best teachers, with other people's experiences not far behind. Experienced organisers talk to each other, and share their knowledge.

I hope that this book will share some of mine.

Peter Cotterell

UK AND OVERSEAS TRADE ASSOCIATIONS

UK

Association of British Professional Conference Organisers (ABPCO)
54 Church Street
Tisbury
Salisbury
Wilts SP3 6NH
Tel. 0747 870490
Secretary: Tony Waters

Association of Conference Executives (ACE)
Riverside House
High Street
Huntingdon
Cambs PE18 6SG
Tel. 0480 457595
General Manager: Peter Worger

Association of National Tourist Office Representatives (ANTOR)
42D Compayne Gardens
London NW6 3RY
Tel. 071 624 5817
Secretary: Phyllis Chapman

British Association of Conference Towns (BACT)
1st Floor, Elizabeth House
22 Suffolk Street
Queensway
Birmingham B1 1LS
Tel. 021 616 1400
Director: Tony Rogers

British Universities Accommodation Consortium (BUAC)
Box 208
University Park
Nottingham NG2 2RD
Tel. 0602 504571
Secretary General: Carole Formon

Corporate Hospitality Association (CHA)
PO Box 67
Kingswood
Tadworth
Surrey KY20 6LG
Tel. 0737 833963
Director: Jean Lee

Higher Education Accommodation Consortium (HEAC CONNECT)
36 Collegiate Crescent
Sheffield
Yorks S10 2BP
Tel. 0742 683759
Secretary: Terry Billingham

Meetings Industry Association (MIA)
4 Chantry Gardens
Bourton-on-the-Hill
Moreton-in-the-Marsh
Glos. GL56 9AP
Tel. 0386 700956
Director: Peter Chester

**National Outdoor Events
Association (NOEA)**
7 Hamilton Way
Wallington
Surrey SM6 9NJ
Tel. 081 669 8121
General Secretary: John Barton

**The Event Suppliers
Association (TESA)**
29 Market Place
Wantage
Oxon OX12 8BG
Tel. 0235 772207
Director Jim Winship

Overseas

**Association Internationale
des Palais de Congrés (AIPC)**
Auditorium della Tecnica
Viale Luigi Pasteur 6
100144 Rome
Italy
Tel. 010 396 5916857
Sec. General: Massimo
  Gattamelata

**European Federation of
Conference Towns
(EFCT)**
Helsinki-Finland Congres
  Bureau
Fabianinkatu 4B11
ST00130 Helsinki
Finland
Tel. 010 3580 170688
President: Tuula Lindberg

**International Association of
Professional Congress
Organisers (IAPCO)**
40 Rue Washington
B1050 Brussels
Belgium
Tel. 010 322 6401808
Executive Secretary: Ghislaine
  De Coninck

**International Congress &
Convention Association UK &
Ireland (ICCA)**
c/o Concorde Services Ltd
10 Wendell Rd
London W12 9RT
Tel. 081 743 3106
Chairman: Sarah Frost-Wellings

**Meeting Planners
International (MPI)**
1950 Stemmons Freeway
Suite 5018
Dallas
Texas 75207-3109
USA
Tel. 1(214) 712-7701
Chief Executive Officer: Edwin
  Griffin Jnr.

UK AND OVERSEAS TRADE PUBLICATIONS

UK

ACE NEWSLETTER
Association of Conference Executives
Riverside House
High Street
Huntingdon
Cambs PE18 6SG
Tel. 0480 457595

ASSOCIATION MEETINGS INTERNATIONAL
Conference & Travel
  Publications Ltd
Media House
The Square
Forest Row
Sussex RH18 5EP
Tel. 0342 824044

CONFERENCE & EXHIBITION FACT FINDER
Batiste Publications Ltd
Pembroke House
Campsbourne Road
Hornsey
London N8 7PE

CONFERENCE & INCENTIVE TRAVEL
Haymarket Business
  Publications
30 Lancaster Gate
London W2 3LP
Tel. 071 413 4307

DELEGATES
Professional Meetings Ltd
Premier House
10 Greycoat Place
Victoria
London SW1P 1SB
Tel. 071 222 8866

EVENT ORGANISER
The Event Suppliers Association
29 Market Place
Wantage
Oxfordshire OX12 8DG
Tel. 0235 772207

INCENTIVE TRAVEL FILE
29a Market Square
Biggleswade
Beds SG18 8AQ
Tel: 0767 316255

MEETINGS & INCENTIVE TRAVEL
Conference & Travel
  Publications.
Media House
The Square
Forest Row
Sussex RG18 5EP
Tel. 0342 824044

MEETINGS FILE
29a Market Square
Biggleswade
Beds SG18 8AQ
Tel: 0767 316255

Overseas

CONFERENCE & INCENTIVE MANAGEMENT
Reichenhaller Strasse 46
D–81547 Munich
Germany

MEETINGS & CONVENTIONS
500 Plaza Drive
Secausus
NJ 07096 USA

SUCCESSFUL MEETINGS
633 3rd Avenue
New York NY 10017
USA

THE MEETINGS MANAGER
1950 Stemmons Freeway
Suite 5018
Dallas
Texas 75207-3109
USA

TW TAGUNGS-WIRTSCHAFT
Mainzer Landstrasse 251
Postfach 101528
D-60326 Frankfurt am Main 1
Germany

APPENDIX THREE ━━━━━

TRAINING COURSES IN CONFERENCE ORGANISATION

ACE International
Riverside House
High Street
Huntingdon
Cambs PE18 6SG
Tel. 0480 457595
General Manager: Peter Worger

Campaign Management Associates
St Georges Place
St Peter port
Guernsey
Channel Islands
Tel. 0481 728007
Director: Tony Carey

The Meetings Forum
29a Market Square
Biggleswade
Beds SG18 8AQ
Tel. 0767 316855
Director: Peter Cotterell

APPENDIX FOUR ━━━

SPEAKER BUREAUX

Celebrity Speakers International Ltd
Studio 230 Canalot
222 Kensal Road
London W10 5BN
Tel. 081 969 9419

The Markethill Group
26 Cairns Road
Westbury Park
Bristol
Avon BS6 7TY
Tel. 0272 249050

Prime Performers Ltd
The Studio
5 Kidderpore Avenue
London WW3 7SX
Tel. 071 431 0211

The Right Address Ltd
The High Barn
Pinner Hill Road
Pinner
Middx HA5 3XQ
Tel. 081 868 1376

GLOSSARY

ACE	Association of Conference Executives.
Bahoo	Video projector – brand name.
Bedroom stock	Quantity of bedrooms available in a destination.
Bio	Biographical details, usually of speaker.
Blackout	Complete darkness for image projection.
Block	To book a number of bedrooms.
Blonde	Type of light.
Break out	Split audience into small groups for workshop sessions.
Bump	To deny a customer accommodation on travel already booked.
Concurrent sessions	Sessions run at the same time as other sessions.
Corkage	Charge made by venue when clients supply own wine, or other drink.
Corp rate	Corporate rate for accommodation given to organisations.
Cover	A table setting for one.
Cut-off	Date by which rooms booked by organiser must be taken up by delegates.
CVB	Convention and Visitor Bureau.
DMC	Destination Management Consultant.
Dry run	Rehearsal.
Facilitator	Person who leads a discussion, interactive session or training session.
Fam trip	Familiarisation visit – also inspection visit.
Feedback	Opinions of participants regarding conference and/or venue. Also the loud shriek produced when a microphone is used too close to a speaker.
Function sheet	Document used by hotel to list all requirements of conference.
GM	General Manager.
Grockles	Disparaging term used by tourism industry to describe customers.
Ground handlers	Overseas agents who handle transportation side once delegates have reached destination.

Hold harmless	Clause in contract which absolves of responsibility.
Housekeeping announcements	Announcements made to delegates, usually at the beginning of the event, covering such aspects as the programme, break times, message arrangements, etc.
ICO	Independent Conference Organiser
Keynote	Speech, usually the first, which sets the theme for the event. Speaker giving this is the keynoter.
Low season	The time when a destination receives its lowest number of visitors.
Meet 'n' greet	(USA) The first contact delegates will have with reception staff.
MIA	Meetings Industry Association.
MPI	Meeting Planners International.
No-show	Someone who doesn't turn up for an event, or to take a booked hotel room, or flight.
PCO	Professional Conference Organiser
Peak season	Time when a destination receives its highest number of visitors.
Pick-up	Number of delegates booking accommodation at the offered rate. Also called **Take up**.
Plenary	A session attended by all delegates.
Poster session	Display of reports or scientific/academic papers put up by authors.
Rack	The venue's highest published rate.
Raked	Seating arranged in steps, as in a theatre.
Redhead	A type of light.
Rooming list	A list of delegates and the accommodation required for each.
Rounds	Round banqueting tables, usually holding 8–10.
Shoulder season	Time between the low and peak seasons at a destination.
Speaker support	Range of audiovisual aids used by speakers.
Syndicate group	Small workshop-style group, usually 2–10 participants.
Thematics	The art of theming.
Throw	The distance an image is projected.
Turn round	Cleaning and alteration of a room between events.
Walk in	Guest that walks into hotel and registers without booking, often paying the lowest price.